Speak to Win

How to Present with Power in Any Situation

Brian Tracy

American Management Association

New York • Atlanta • Brussels • Chicago • Mexico City • San Francisco
Shanghai • Tokyo • Toronto • Washington, D.C.

Special discounts on bulk quantities of AMACOM books are available to corporations, professional associations, and other organizations. For details, contact Special Sales Department, AMACOM, a division of American Management Association, 1601 Broadway, New York, NY 10019.
Tel: 212–903–8316. Fax: 212–903–8083.
E-mail: specialsls@amanet.org
Website: www.amacombooks.org/go/specialsales
To view all AMACOM titles go to: www.amacombooks.org

This publication is designed to provide accurate and authoritative information in regard to the subject matter covered. It is sold with the understanding that the publisher is not engaged in rendering legal, accounting, or other professional service. If legal advice or other expert assistance is required, the services of a competent professional person should be sought.

Library of Congress Cataloging-in-Publication Data

Tracy, Brian.
    Speak to win : how to present with power in any situation / Brian Tracy.
        p.   cm.
    Includes index.
    ISBN-13: 978–0-8144–0157–6
    ISBN-10: 0–8144–0157–0
    1. Public speaking. I. Title.

    PN4129.15.T73   2008
    808.5′1—dc22

                                                                        2007043407

Printing number

10   9   8   7

This book is fondly dedicated to my wife, Barbara, who has been with me and supported me over the years while I have been traveling and speaking all over the world. She has been a loyal and understanding partner, friend, and wonderful mother. Without her, nothing would have been possible, and with her support, there have been no limits.

Contents

Speaking to Win

Our destiny changes with our thoughts; we shall become what we wish to become, do what we wish to do, when our habitual thoughts correspond with our desires.

—ORISON SWETT MARDEN

Your ability to speak to an audience is essential to your success. Speaking well can garner the respect and esteem of others, make you more valuable to your company, and get attention from people who can help you and open doors for you. Good speaking ability will also convince people that you are generally more talented and intelligent than others who do not speak as well.

What is your most valuable asset? Your *mind*. One of the most precious skills you have is your ability to think well and to express yourself clearly. This skill can help you earn more and get pro-

1

moted faster as much as any other talent you can develop. After all, the only way you can demonstrate your mastery of a subject is by expressing your thoughts and ideas clearly aloud and in writing. When you speak well, people say, "He really knows what he's talking about."

The good news is that your mind is like a muscle. It grows stronger and more capable with use. Organizing your thoughts and words in advance makes you more alert and aware of what you are saying and how you are saying it. The act of planning, preparing, and delivering talks and presentations forces you to use your mind at a higher level, and it actually makes you smarter.

Eliminate Your Fear and Turbocharge Your Career

Some years ago, I gave a one-day seminar on executive effectiveness to a group of businesspeople. During the talk I emphasized the importance of being able to speak well and influence people in business.

At the end of the day, a somewhat shy businessman came up to me and told me that, as a result of my comments, he had decided that he was going to learn how to be a good speaker. He was tired of being ignored by his supervisors and passed over for promotions.

A year later, I received a letter from him telling me his story. He had immediately taken action on his resolution. He joined a local chapter of Toastmasters and began attending weekly meetings. At each meeting, each member was required to stand up and speak on some subject, and each person was given a grade at the end of the meeting.

Toastmasters uses the process of "systematic desensitization."

This means that if you do something over and over, you finally become desensitized to it. When you speak repeatedly in front of others, you eventually lose your fears and misgivings.

He also took a Dale Carnegie course for 14 weeks. At each session, he was required to speak in front of his peers. Within six months, he had given so many long and short presentations to friendly groups of peers that most of his fear and anxiety about speaking was gone. In its place was a growing confidence in his ability to express himself to an audience.

Doors Open for You

At about this point in his growth and development, there was a small emergency at his engineering firm. One of the partners had been scheduled to give a presentation to the members of a client company. But the partner was ill and unable to make the meeting. The businessman's boss asked him if he would prepare and present the company's proposal instead. He accepted the assignment.

He prepared thoroughly throughout the evening and the following morning. He then went to the client's office, made an excellent presentation for the firm's services, and got the business. When he returned to the office, his boss told him that the president of the prospective client had called and thanked him for sending someone to give such an excellent presentation of the firm's services.

Within a few weeks, he was being sent out regularly to call on the firm's prospects and clients. He was promoted, and then promoted again. Soon he was a member of senior management and on his way to becoming a partner. He told me that his whole life changed by making a decision to become a good speaker and following up that decision with specific actions.

Increase Your Self-Esteem

Becoming an excellent public speaker will help you in every part of your career. But there is an even more important reason to learn to speak well to an audience. Psychologists tell us that your level of self-esteem, or "how much you like yourself," largely determines the quality of your inner and outer life.

The better and more persuasively you speak, the more you like yourself. The more you like yourself, the more optimistic and confident you are. The more you like yourself, the more positive and personable you are in your relationships with others. The more you like yourself, the healthier, happier, and more positive you become in everything you do.

Improve Your Self-Image

When you learn to speak effectively, your self-image improves as well. Your self-image is your "inner mirror." It's the way you see yourself and think about yourself prior to and during any event. The more positive your self-image, the more competent your performance. The very act of visualizing yourself performing at your best prior to any event or activity will improve your performance.

We are all highly sensitive to the thoughts, feelings, and especially the respect of others. Somerset Maugham wrote, "Everything we do in life is to earn the respect of others, or at the very least, not to lose their respect." So when you speak well, your audience likes and respects you more. As a result, you like and respect yourself more as well. When you get positive feedback from others as the result of speaking well, your self-image improves. You see yourself and think about yourself in a more positive way. You develop a sense of personal power. You walk, talk, and act with greater confidence.

Excellent Speaking Is Learnable

Perhaps the best news about speaking to groups is that it is a learnable skill. Most people who are competent speakers today at one time could not lead silent prayer in a phone booth. Many people who appear confident and articulate in front of an audience were at one time terrified at the idea of standing up and speaking in public.

Your goal should be to be in the top 10 percent of communicators. And you should continually remind yourself that almost everyone who is in the top 10 percent today started in the bottom 10 percent. Everyone who is doing well was once doing poorly. As Harv Eker says, "Every master was once a disaster."

You have probably heard it said that practice makes perfect. Some people go even further and say that perfect practice makes perfect. However, the truth is that *imperfect* practice makes perfect.

On your journey to mastering the art of speaking to an audience, you will make many small and large mistakes. You will often feel nervous and inadequate. You will say the wrong things and forget to say the right things. You will mumble and stumble and wonder if you will ever get it right.

Move out of Your Comfort Zone

But in order to achieve excellence in speaking or in any field, you must be willing to move out of your comfort zone and into your discomfort zone. You must be willing to feel clumsy and awkward during your growth and development if you are ever going to move to a higher level of competence.

You may remember the story of the famous Greek orator, Demosthenes, considered one of the finest speakers of antiquity. When he began, he was nervous, shy, and troubled by both a stutter and a speech impediment. But he was determined to be a good speaker. To overcome his difficulties, he put pebbles in his mouth and spoke loudly to the sea for hours every day. In time, he eliminated his stutter and overcame his speech impediment. His voice grew louder, stronger, and more confident. He became one of the greatest orators in history.

If you are a beginning speaker, this book will show you how to accelerate the process of speaking with competence, confidence, and clarity. If you are a more experienced speaker, this book will give you some of the most powerful techniques, tactics, and methods of great speakers in every area of business, politics, and personal life.

The Four Ds to Speaking Excellence

To become an outstanding speaker, you simply must have the four Ds.

1. *Desire.* First, you must have an intense, burning *desire* to speak well. If your desire is strong enough and you want to achieve speaking mastery long enough, nothing can stop you from reaching your goal. But desire is not enough.
2. *Decision.* You must make a *decision* this very day that you are going to make every effort, overcome any obstacle, and do whatever it takes to become excellent.
3. *Discipline.* You must have the *discipline* to plan, prepare, and deliver talks and presentations, over and over again, until you achieve mastery. There are no shortcuts to hard work in developing an essential skill.
4. *Determination.* Finally, you must have the *determination* to

persist and persevere in spite of any short-term setback, obstacle, or embarrassment you may experience.

The Only Limit Is You

Our greatest enemies are always our own doubts and fears. But there are no limits to what you can do, be, or have except for the limits you place on yourself.

Over the years, I have delivered more than 4,000 presentations and spoken personally to more than 5,000,000 people in 46 countries. In the pages ahead, I will take you by the hand and show you, step by step, how to develop the courage, confidence, and competence to be a winning speaker in any situation.

CHAPTER 1

The Arts of Speaking and Rhetoric

All his oratorical efforts were made for practical effect. He never spoke merely to be heard.

—ABRAHAM LINCOLN, in his eulogy on Henry Clay

Throughout history, the height of human effectiveness has been the ability to persuade others. As such, the aim or goal of public speaking is to cause an action to take place that would not have taken place in the absence of the words of the speaker. For example, when Demosthenes spoke, people said, "What a fine speaker he is." But when Alcibiades spoke, they said, "Let us march!"

Your job as a speaker is to motivate and impel your listeners to think, feel, and act differently as the result of your words. It is to make them take action of some kind. It is to motivate them to "march!"

Fortunately, becoming a master speaker and business communicator is a learnable skill. If you can learn how to drive a car, type on a keyboard, or use a cell phone, you can become an effective speaker and change not only your life, but the lives of your listeners.

The Three Elements of Persuasion

Aristotle was the first major philosopher to recognize the importance of rhetoric as an essential tool of the leader. He broke down the essential elements of persuasion into three parts: *logos* (logic), *ethos* (ethic), and *pathos* (emotion). Let us take each of them in turn.

Logos refers to the logic, the words, and the reasons in your argument. It is important that everything that you say fits together like links in a chain or pieces of a jigsaw puzzle to form a coherent statement or argument. When you think through and plan your talk, you organize your various points in a sequence from the general to the particular, from the start to the conclusion, with each point building on each previous point to form a persuasive argument.

The second aspect of persuasion is *ethos.* This refers to your character, ethics, and your believability when you speak. Increasing your credibility with your audience before and during your speech increases the likelihood that listeners will accept your arguments and take action on your recommendations.

The third aspect of persuasion is *pathos.* This is the emotional content of your argument and is perhaps the most important. It is only when you connect emotionally and move people at a funda-mental level that you can motivate them to change their thinking and take a particular action.

All three elements—logos, ethos, and pathos—must be woven together if you want to move people and persuade them to your point of view.

The Three Components of Your Message

Albert Mehrabian of UCLA conducted a series of studies into ef-fective communication some years ago. He concluded that there are three components of any spoken message: the words, the tone of voice, and the speaker's body language.

The Words

Surprisingly, according to Mehrabian, the words count for only 7 percent of the message conveyed. Of course, the words you use are vitally important and must be selected with care. They must be organized in a proper sequence and be grammatically correct. But everyone has heard a boring, academic speaker whose words were brilliant but whose message fell flat. The words alone are not enough.

The Tone

The second element of communication that Mehrabian identified was the tone of voice. In his calculation, 38 percent of the message is contained in the speaker's tonality and emphasis on various words.

Recite the sentence "I love you very much." By putting the emphasis on any one of those words or by making the sentence a question rather than a statement, you can change the entire meaning of the sentence. Try it. Make your tone reflect a sincere statement or a question. Notice how the meaning can be completely different just by focusing on a single word.

Every man has had the experience of arguing with the woman in his life over a simple subject. Because men tend to use words as tools and women tend to use words for understanding and relationship building, they hear the same words differently. For example, she might become angry or hurt at something he said. He will respond by saying, "But I just said such and such."

She will reply angrily, "It wasn't what you said; it was the way you said it."

By deliberately changing your tone of voice and being aware of how important it is, you can change the entire message and the subsequent effect it has on your listeners.

The Body

Mehrabian also found that fully 55 percent of the message is contained in the speaker's body language. This is because there are 22 times as many nerves from the eye to the brain as from the ear to the brain.

For this reason, visual impressions are very powerful.

Be Aware of Your Style of Communication

Excellent communicators always pay attention to the effect their body language has on the level of acceptance of the message they are trying to convey.

When your arms hang loosely at your side, with your palms outward and open, and you look directly at the audience with a smile as you speak, your listeners relax and absorb your message like a sponge absorbs water. If your face is serious and unsmiling, with your arms folded or gripping the lectern, your listeners respond as if an angry parent is scolding them. They close up and become defensive, resisting your message and your attempt to persuade them to think and act in a particular way. Body language is very important!

Because I have given so many talks to so many audiences, speakers continually ask me for my comments on a talk or seminar that they have just delivered. I am always reluctant to give critical feedback because people in general seem to be hypersensitive to comments that are not glowing and positive. Nonetheless, it is amazing how often I give the same piece of advice: "Slow down, pause, and smile between points and sentences."

It is equally amazing how many speakers take this advice and notice an immediate and positive difference in the way their audiences respond to them. When you slow down, your words are clearer and you appear more articulate. Your tone of voice is more pleasant and enjoyable. And when you smile, you radiate warmth, friendliness, and acceptance. This causes your audience to relax and become more open to your message. We'll talk more about this in Chapter 8.

A Simple Structure for Short Talks

There is a simple three-part structure that you can use to design any speech. You can use this model for a one-minute talk or for a 30-minute talk.

Part One

Part one is the opening. You simply tell the audience what you are going to say in your speech. For example, you could say: "Thank you for being here. In the next few minutes, I want to tell you about the three problems facing our industry today and the actions we can take to turn them to our advantage in the months ahead."

This opening sets the stage, prepares the audience, and gives your speech a track to run on.

Part Two

The second part is to tell them what you promised in the opening. This can consist of one, two, or three points. If it is a short speech, it should only include three key points developed in a sequence. For example, you might say: "We are facing increased competition, shrinking profit margins, and changing customer tastes. Let us look at each of these, in order, and consider alternative ways of dealing with them effectively."

Part Three

The third part of speaking is a summary of what you just told the audience. You should never expect your listeners to memorize everything that you have said the first time they hear it. Looking back, summarizing and repeating is helpful and enjoyable for your audience. For example, you could say:

> To summarize, to deal with increased competition, we must improve the quality of our offerings and the speed at which we deliver them to our customers. To deal with shrinking markets, we must expand into new markets and increase our product offerings to attract new customers. To deal with changing customer tastes, we must develop and market products and services that our customers want today, rather than what they may have wanted in the past.

With our joint commitment to these three goals, we will not only survive but thrive in the exciting times ahead. Thank you.

You Have a Job to Do

Peggy Noonan, speechwriter for Ronald Reagan, once wrote, "Every speech has a job to do."

One of the most important things you must do, before you speak, is start with the end in mind. Determine what you want your talk to accomplish. Ask yourself what I call the "objective question": "If they interviewed people after my talk and asked them, 'What did you get from this speech and what are you going to do differently as a result?' what would I want them to say?" Everything in your speech, from your opening through the body to your closing remarks, should aim at achieving this goal.

When I work with corporate clients, I ask them the "objective question." I also ask them why they are inviting me to speak and what objective or objectives they want me to accomplish with their audience. We then discuss and agree on exactly how we want the audience to think, feel, and act after the talk or seminar. Once we are both clear, I will then design the talk or seminar, from beginning to end, to ensure that we achieve that result. You can do the same.

A Complex Structure for Longer Speeches

In designing a longer talk, there is a more complex structure that you can use. It consists of the following eight parts, each of which I will develop and explain in the pages ahead.

1. *The Opening*. The purpose of the opening is to get the audience's attention, build expectations, and focus listeners on

the speaker. There is no point in talking if no one is listening or paying attention.

2. *The Introduction.* This is where you tell the audience what is coming and why it is important.
3. *The First Point.* This is where you transition into the body of your talk. Your first point sets the stage and begins to deliver on your initial promise.
4. *The Transition into the Next Point.* You must make it clear that you have finished with one point and are now moving on to another. This is an art in and of itself.
5. *The Second Key Point.* This point should follow logically from your first point.
6. *Another Transition.* Here you make it clear that you are moving onward to another subject.
7. *The Third Key Point.* This flows naturally from the first two points and begins moving you toward the end of your talk.
8. *The Summary.* This is your conclusion and call to action.

In Chapter 2, you will learn how to organize and develop your talk so that you achieve each of these goals in the proper order and sequence.

In learning to speak effectively, there is no substitute for practice, especially practicing aloud. Over the years, I have observed hundreds of talks given by both amateurs and professionals, and you can always tell when they have been practiced thoroughly beforehand.

Speaking with Power and Presence

The popular author Elbert Hubbard was once asked how one became a writer. He replied, "The only way to learn to write is to write and write and write and write and write and write and write."

Likewise, to learn the art of speaking, the only way to learn is to speak and speak and speak and speak and speak and speak and speak. Learning to speak is like learning any other skill. It requires practice and repetition until you have mastered the ability to communicate and persuade.

One of the best ways to improve your speaking style and ability is to recite poetry aloud. Memorize a poem that you enjoy, one with a great story and wonderful lines, and then recite it over and over again. Each time you recite this poem aloud, put energy and passion into your voice. Vary the rhythm and tone and emphasis on the various words. Imagine that you are auditioning for a major role in a big-budget movie that will make you rich and famous. Deliver the lines of this poem as though it is extremely important that you connect emotionally and enthusiastically with the listener.

When you read good poetry, you not only learn how to develop sentences, but you also learn how to use a wider variety of words to make your points more effectively. The rule is this: People will forget what you said, but they will remember how you said it. As you change the emphasis from word to word and from sentence to sentence, you develop an almost musical ability to speak in such a way that listeners are caught up in your message.

Another great exercise is to read Shakespeare, especially the famous monologues from *Hamlet, Macbeth, Julius Caesar,* and *Romeo and Juliet.* When you read these wonderful monologues and soliloquies, you expand your command of language and your competence in rhetoric and persuasion.

Learning from Others

One of the very best ways to become a better speaker is to listen to as many other speakers as possible. Take notes. Observe how they walk, talk, move, and gesture. Observe how an experienced speaker opens a talk; transitions into the body of the talk; uses examples, illustrations, and humor; wraps up the talk; and concludes her time with the audience.

Make a list of the points you want to observe, from the opening to the close, and give the speaker a grade from 1 to 10 for each of those points. Think about how he or she could have done each thing better and how you could do it better yourself.

Listen to some of the best speeches ever given, many of which are available on CD. Play them over and over and notice how the speaker uses logos, ethos, and pathos to persuade the listener to think, feel, and act differently.

Summary

The wonderful thing about communication is that you cannot get worse at it by doing it. To master the arts of speaking and rhetoric, you must be prepared to learn and practice, over and over again, for months and even years. There are no shortcuts.

It is also important to remember that preparation is what separates mediocrity from greatness. So spend time developing your logic, planning your words, and working toward your goal for your audience. And practice. Every new line of poetry that you remember and recite, every monologue that you deliver aloud, every speaker that you observe and critique increases your ability to become an excellent speaker yourself. There are no limits.

CHAPTER 2

Planning and Preparation Made Simple

The true worth of a man is to be measured in the objects he pursues.
—MARCUS AURELIUS

Fully 90 percent of your success as a speaker will be determined by how well you plan your speech.

Ernest Hemingway once wrote, "You must know ten words for every word you write, or the reader will know that this is not a true thing." In speaking, however, you must read and research *100 words* for every word you speak, or the listener will know that you are speaking off the top of your head. The listener will immediately sense that you lack a depth of knowledge in your subject unless you are not only prepared but overprepared.

Poor preparation before an intelligent, discerning audience automatically downgrades your credibility—your ethos. If you are unprepared, or even worse, if you tell listeners that you are "not an expert on this subject," they immediately turn off to your message, no matter how good it is.

On the other hand, excellent preparation is immediately obvious. It increases your credibility. Preparation impresses your listeners and makes them more open and receptive to your message.

Start with Audience Demographics and Characteristics

The starting point of preparation is your audience. Remember, it is not about you; it is about *them*.

Begin as if you were a market researcher and you are determined to understand your customers fully. Who are they exactly? Who will be in the audience? This is the key to an effective talk and to excellent preparation. Here are some demographic particulars that you can use to tailor your speeches.

Age and Age Range

How old are your audience members and what are their age ranges? Younger audiences have different understandings, different cultural knowledge, and different backgrounds from older audiences. Knowing their age is very important.

Gender

What is the gender mix in your audience? Sometimes my audiences will be 50:50 males and females. Sometimes my audiences will be 95 percent men or 95 percent women. This gender break-down will influence how you design your remarks and make your points.

Income

What are the incomes of the people in your audiences? How much do they earn on average? What is their income range, from the lowest to the highest? In particular, how do they earn their incomes, and what influences those incomes? Knowing this can help you to refer to money and income-related topics in a way that it is more acceptable to more of your listeners.

Education

What is the educational background of the people in your audience? Are they high school graduates? Are they university graduates? Do they have liberal-arts degrees or engineering degrees? Knowing the type of education your listeners have helps you choose relevant examples, illustrations, and vocabulary.

Occupation

What do your audience members do for a living? How long have they been working in their particular fields? What is happening in their particular fields today? Is this a boom time or a bust time for the work that they do?

Family Status

What is the family status of your audience? Are audience members married, single, divorced, or widowed? Are they mostly married or mostly single? Do most have children? These are essential facts for you to discover.

Audience Familiarity with Your Subject

What is the audience's familiarity with your subject? How much does it already know about what you will be saying? Are audience members beginners, or are they somewhat knowledgeable? This will decide how complex or simple you make your talk.

How Do They Think?

Analyze what your audience members think by asking these questions:

- What are their goals and aspirations?
- What are their hopes and fears as they relate to your subject?
- What needs do they have that you can fulfill with your comments and your ideas?
- What are their values and beliefs?
- What is their political orientation?
- What sort of religious feelings or commitments do they have?
- What are their worries, concerns, or problems?

Understanding the emotional context people bring to your talk can be very helpful in connecting with them. Asking meeting planners these questions in advance and studying their websites and published materials will help you get the answers you need.

Common Desires

It is important to understand what dreams, goals, or ideas unite your audience. Let me give you an example. I speak to many audiences of sales professionals, entrepreneurs, business owners, and network marketers. The common denominator is that they all want to be financially successful. Therefore, everything I talk about relates to how they can use certain ideas to increase their incomes and their profitability. As a result of taking this approach, my audiences lean forward, listen closely to every word I speak, and often give me standing ovations. You can do the same.

What Is Happening in Their Lives?

Once I was booked to speak for a large national corporation that sold its products through retailers and distributors across the country. I was brought in to speak just after the organization's executives had made a major announcement. The announcement was that in 30 days the company was going to begin selling its products directly to customers, and it was going to do so at the same prices that the salespeople would be offering. The difference was that the company would credit the sales commissions it would normally pay to its salespeople back to the customers if they bought directly from the factory.

As you can imagine, the salespeople in the audience were in a mild state of shock. Their entire lives and incomes were dependent upon the commissions they earned from selling through the distributor network. Now, with the change in company policy, the distributor network could purchase directly from the company at the same prices or with commissions credited back. The salespeople had had the chair kicked out from underneath them.

The company brought me in and paid my fee to motivate the salespeople to go out and work harder in any case, even though their primary source of income had been dramatically diminished.

I still remember looking out at the audience. They looked stunned and unbelieving. They looked at me as though I were an enemy, conjured up by the corporation, to smooth over what the company had just done to hurt them in their pocketbooks. Because I knew all of this, I was at least prepared to speak effectively to an unresponsive and, in many cases, negative audience. It pays to take the time to find out what is going on in the company or group.

Do Your Homework—Go Beyond Demographics and Traits

When you are speaking to people in a specific industry, business association, or other organization, you must find out everything you can about what is going on professionally with those people before you get up to speak. Is the market good or bad for what they are selling? Are they growing, staying flat, or are they declining in the current market? What are the business and political trends that are affecting them at this moment? Here are some other things to check on when planning a speech or presentation.

Consider What's Happening in Their Businesses

I was once called in to speak to a large group of managers of a major multinational corporation. The company had just announced a series of layoffs of managers at all levels, and I was speaking to the survivors. However, just before I arrived to give my talk on personal productivity and leadership effectiveness, the company announced even more management layoffs and that many of the people in the audience would be cut within the next 30 days. As a result, my audience was less than responsive and enthusiastic. The only things that listeners could think of while I was talking was that they might be next. This is not a good situation. But it is essential that you know about it. Take the time to find out.

Find Out What the Local Environment Is Like

Know what is going on in the city in which you are speaking. For example, in several cases, I've spoken in cities where the local team either won or lost a championship within the last day or two. It is important that you are aware of this and that you mention it in your introductory remarks. Otherwise, the audience will often be preoccupied with the sporting event and will feel that you are an outsider who does not know or understand them.

Keep in Mind Who Else They've Heard Lately

Another part of preparation is to learn about your audience's other experiences with speakers. Who else has spoken to this audience and on what subjects? How did listeners react to the other speakers and to their subjects? Did they like what they heard? Were they disappointed with a previous speaker? If so, why? If they liked the previous speaker, what was the reason? What did he or she say?

At a longer meeting, it's important to know who will be speaking before you. What subjects will they speak on? You should also know who spoke to the audience at the last meeting and how it reacted to those speeches.

Tailor Your Talk to the Audience's Specific Concerns

Recently, I was speaking to a group of 4,000 people. I spent considerable time preparing my remarks, based on in-depth discussions with the key meeting organizers. As a result, my 90-minute talk wove all the main company themes, concerns, competitive challenges, and future directions into a single fabric.

After the talk, the president of the company took me aside and told me that this was one of the best talks she had ever heard. The company had hired previous speakers, at high rates, who had promised to customize and tailor their remarks to the audience but had made no effort at all to do so. She said it was immediately obvious when they began speaking that they had spent little time incorporating the company's concerns into their speeches. As a result, they were never invited back.

Start with the End in Mind

Remember the "objective question." If you could interview the audience participants afterward and ask, "What did you learn from my talk, and what are you going to do differently as a result?" what would you want them to say? The more specific you can be regarding your answer to this question the easier it will be for you to design and structure your remarks so that you achieve this objective in the time allotted.

Watch the Clock

In addition, you must be absolutely clear about the amount of time you have and the expected structure of the talk. Sometimes, audiences expect you to speak for 75 percent of the time and then conduct a question-and-answer session afterward. In other cases, the meeting planner will want you to speak for the whole time. In either case, it is important that you end exactly when you say you will.

Many talks, conferences, and meetings are carefully choreographed with regard to time. For example, once I was invited to give a talk at a meeting of 5,000 people. The meeting planners were so fastidious that they asked me to write out the talk in detail, and then they paid me to present my talk to a small group of executives who would advise me and comment on the talk. Their primary concern was the exact number of minutes I would use.

When I gave the talk, the speaker before me, who had been allocated 22 minutes, spoke for 28 minutes. As I stood behind the stage, waiting for my turn to go on, I noticed that the meeting planners were beside themselves with stress, anxiety, and anger. They did not even care what the speaker said. All they cared about was that he was complicating their schedule by speaking longer than he had promised. He was never invited back.

Once You've Done Your Homework, Prepare

There is a powerful method of preparation that I have used over the years. I start with a clean sheet of paper. I write the title of my talk at the top. I then write a one-sentence description of the purpose or objective of the talk. What is the "job" it has to do? Then, I discipline myself to do a "down dump" of every single idea, insight, phrase, statistic, example, or illustration that I could possibly use in the talk. I write and write and write and write.

Sometimes, I end up with two or three pages of notes. From those notes, I will then begin selecting particular elements and putting them in a logical sequence so that they make up a talk that flows from beginning to end. You can do the same. It is amazing how many ideas you will come up with when you force yourself to write 20 or 30 or 50 points that you feel would be appropriate for a talk.

Once you have all these points organized, go back through with a red pen and circle the points that would have the most impact in your talk. Organize these points in sequence and you will see your talk start to form naturally.

The PREP Formula

Once you have chosen your points, you can use what is called the "PREP" formula for each point that you want to make in your presentation.

P: Point of View

State your thought, idea, or fact at the beginning. For example, you could say: "More people are going to make more money in the next 10 years than in the last 100 years."

R: Reasons

State your reasons for holding this point of view or idea. For example, you might say: "The number of millionaires and billionaires, most of them self-made in one generation, has increased by 60 percent in the last five years, and the rate of increase is accelerating."

E: Example

Illustrate, reinforce, or prove your point of view. For example, you could say: "In 1900, there were 5,000 millionaires in America and no billionaires. By the year 2000, there were 5,000,000 millionaires and more than 500 billionaires. By 2007, according to *BusinessWeek* magazine, there were 8,900,000 millionaires in the

United States and over 700 billionaires worldwide, most of them first-generation."

P: Point of View

Restate the first "P" to emphasize your idea. For example, you might say: "There have never been more opportunities for you, the creative minority, to achieve financial success than exist today—except for tomorrow and the years ahead."

The PREP Formula in Action

Here is an example of how the PREP formula comes together:

> This is the very best time in human history to be alive *(point of view)*. We have the highest rate of home ownership, the lowest level of unemployment, and the fastest growing economy in the industrialized world *(reasons)*. Last year alone, more than 1,000,000 Americans started their own businesses and launched onto the seas of entrepreneurship to take advantage of the current economy *(example)*. Because this is such a great time, more people are going to make more money in the years ahead than in the last 100 years put together *(restate point of view)*.

You can organize every key point of your talk using this simple formula. It is incredibly powerful and influential in persuading your audience to accept your message.

The Windshield-Wiper Method

You can use the "windshield-wiper" method as well in designing your talk. As you know, you have both a right brain and a left brain. Your left brain is activated by facts and information. Your right brain is activated by feelings, stories, quotes, and examples.

The way you use this method is simple: You state a fact and follow it with a story. State another fact and follow it with a quote. State another fact and follow it with an example. State a fact and follow it with a numerical illustration. You go back and forth, like a windshield wiper.

To use this method of preparation, take a sheet of paper and draw a line down the center. On the left side of the line, you write the fact or point that you wish to make. On the right side, you write the example, story, or illustration that proves or demonstrates the fact. For each item on the left-hand column, you have a fact or story on the right-hand column.

When you give a talk using this method, you will activate both the left and right brains of everyone in your audience. They will lean forward and hang on every word. You will keep them totally engaged the entire time.

The Circles Method

To plan your talk on paper, you can use a picture or a visual illustration. What I do is draw a series of five large circles down the center of a page. Each circle represents an element of the talk. The first circle will be the introduction and the comments that I will use to get attention and to set the stage. The second, third, and fourth circles will be the key points that I intend to make. The fifth circle will be the wrap-up and close.

If I am giving a longer talk, I sometimes have seven circles down the page, and I even use another page if necessary. In each case, the first and last circles are my opening and closing. The middle circles are the key points I plan to make in an orderly sequence.

Plan Your Opening and Closing with Care

Planning your speech's opening is important. Plan your opening word for word, and rehearse it over and over again in your mind, aloud, and in front of a mirror. Your opening comments set the stage, build expectations, and communicate a clear message to your audience. They must not be left to chance.

You should plan your closing comments word for word as well. Think about exactly what you are going to say to wrap up your talk. If for any reason your speech length is cut back because of changes in the schedule, at least you know how to end your talk in an effective way.

Planning the Visual Part of Your Speech

In the course of giving your talk, you should think about the visual elements that you can use to illustrate your points and to make them come alive for the audience.

The Magic-Wand Technique

One of these elements is what I call the "Magic-Wand" technique. As I am speaking, I will take a gold pen out of my pocket and say something that incorporates the pen, such as, "Imagine that you could wave a magic wand over this situation and make it perfect in every way. What would it look like?"

I wave the "magic wand" and pause to allow each person to imagine what this situation would look like if it were perfect. I then discuss a series of strategies and techniques that the listeners can use to improve their current situation.

PowerPoint in Speaking

Whether you use PowerPoint depends upon many factors. In the professional speaking industry, there is an expression: "Death by PowerPoint." Many speakers have started to rely on PowerPoint presentations so heavily that their personalities and the essence of their talks get lost as they go from point to point on the screen.

If you are going to use PowerPoint, which can be ideal in certain situations, it is best to follow a few rules.

The 5 X 5 Rule

First and foremost, you should never have more than five lines on a slide, and each line should never have more than five words. Any more than this can distract and even confuse your audience. With a smaller room or group, you can use more lines or words than the rule permits.

Regardless of how many points you use, bring them up one at a time as you are commenting on them. Don't make the mistake of bringing up the entire slide full of information so that the audience is busy reading and not paying any attention to you.

Not long ago, when I spoke for a multinational company, the president spoke to the audience for an hour before it was my turn to speak. His PowerPoint presentation consisted of a single slide with hundreds of numbers in rows and columns, none of which were clear to anybody in the audience. He spoke to the screen, commenting on the numbers for a full hour. Because he was the president, everyone in the audience sat politely, but it was excruciatingly painful for all the participants. Don't let this happen to you.

Face the Audience

Second, face the audience when you use PowerPoint. You should have your laptop in front of you illustrating what is appearing on the screen behind you. As you click through your PowerPoint presentation, keep your eyes on the audience members and speak to them the whole time.

When you are not referring to a point on the screen, push the ''B'' on your laptop to blank out the screen. Remember, your face is the most important element in any presentation, and while there are words on the screen, people's eyes will be darting from your face to the screen and back again, like spectators at a tennis game.

Lights, Please

When you use PowerPoint, it is essential that your face be well lit throughout. I am continually dismayed at the number of times that I see senior executives allow themselves to be put in the dark in order to ensure maximum clarity for the projector and the screen. The senior executive, who has traveled a great distance and invested a good deal of time in this presentation, is often standing in the dark, difficult for the audience to see or relate to.

PowerPoint Is Only a Prop

Only use PowerPoint as a prop or as a support. It should not be the main focus of the talk. You are the main focus of the presentation, and PowerPoint is there merely to assist you and to illustrate your points more clearly to your audience.

When you use PowerPoint, practice and rehearse. Go through a dry run three to five times before you make your presentation. Do a complete dress rehearsal to ensure that the PowerPoint and projector are properly hooked up and working smoothly before you begin.

Expect the Unexpected

You have probably seen situations where the entire talk is built around PowerPoint, and then PowerPoint somehow fails to function. The speaker stands up, begins clicking, and nothing happens. People come running up on the stage to tinker with the machine to try to fix it. They call the technician from somewhere else in the hotel. The entire seminar or presentation grinds to a halt while everyone stands around the stage looking sheepish and foolish. Doing a complete run-through before your presentation will help ensure that this won't happen to you.

Keep the Attention on You and Your Message

In any case, when you use PowerPoint, start off with a strong, clear statement that sets the stage for your talk. You can then use PowerPoint to illustrate critical numbers, points, and relationships. When you have finished using PowerPoint, blank out the screen, and be sure to end with a strong focus on your face and your verbal message.

Planning a Smooth Delivery

Every speaker has three talks for a particular occasion. First, there is the talk that the speaker plans to give. Second, there is the talk that the speaker actually gives when he stands up in front of the audience. Third, there is the talk that the speaker wishes he had given as he thinks about it afterward on the way home.

The very best talk of all is when the talk you planned, the talk you gave, and the talk you wish you had given all turn out to be the same. This gives you a deep sense of pleasure and satisfaction.

Move Seamlessly from Point to Point

In planning and preparing your talk, design your transitions from point to point so that it is clear to the audience that you have finished with one point and you are moving on to the next.

Go over your material repeatedly, and continually look for ways to improve the quality and smooth delivery of your message.

Practice—It Pays Off

Some years ago, I was commissioned to give an important talk to an audience containing people who could book me as a speaker if they were sufficiently impressed. I therefore spent an inordinate amount of time practicing, preparing, and rehearsing my speech, finally reviewing the speech about 50 times before I stood up and gave it to the huge audience at the convention center.

The practice paid off. The speech was recorded on both video and audio tape. It was distributed worldwide and was eventually viewed by tens of thousands of people in multiple languages. Some years later, this speech was rated as one of the twelve best speeches ever given out of more than a thousand speeches to this particular organization over a 37-year period. Preparation really paid off.

Use Memory Techniques

Another way that you can prepare yourself to give a great speech is to use a mnemonic. This is where you design your talk in your mind around a particular phrase or series of letters or numbers.

You have probably heard of the mnemonic used by many memory trainers. They will use the word *one* to rhyme with the word *gun*. When they think of their first point, they think of their opening statement coming out of a gun.

They will then use the word *two* to rhyme with the word *shoe*. They will then think of their second point as if it were coming out of a shoe, or under a shoe, or associated with a shoe in some way.

In a like manner, the word *three* rhymes with *tree*, and the speaker will think of his or her third point as hanging from the branches of a tree.

The word *four* rhymes with *door* and the speaker will think of his fourth point as though it were posted on a door.

The word *five* rhymes with the word *hive*, and the speaker will think of her fifth point buzzing around a beehive, and so on.

Six rhymes with *sticks*. *Seven* rhymes with *heaven*. *Eight* rhymes with *gate*. *Nine* rhymes with *tine* (as in a dinner fork), and *ten* rhymes with *hen*.

In each case, by imagining the number and its rhyming symbol, you can connect a part of your talk to it and thus remember ten points in a row without missing a beat. This is a common trick used by speakers who want to stand in front of an audience and speak without notes.

Design Your Talk with a Word

My favorite way of organizing a talk is to build it around a word that is relevant to the talk and important to the audience, such as *success.* You can do this with almost any word. Here is an example of this method of organizing.

The first letter, *S*, stands for *"Sense of purpose."* I then explain the importance of having clear, specific goals before you begin.

The second letter, *U*, stands for *"You are responsible."* I explain that you must take charge of your life and career, and you must refuse to make any excuses.

The third letter, *C*, stands for *"Customer satisfaction."* You must clearly identify your ideal customer, decide what you can do to win her over, and satisfy her better than your competitor can.

The fourth letter, *C*, stands for *"Creativity."* I explain the importance of finding better, faster, cheaper ways to promote and sell your product in today's market.

The fifth letter, *E*, stands for *"Excellence."* You must become absolutely excellent at what you do and continually strive to improve.

The sixth letter, *S*, stands for *"Sensitivity to others."* You must think about other people and how what you do and say can have an effect on them.

Finally, the last letter, *S*, stands for *"Stick to it."* You must resolve in advance that you will never give up and that you will persist in the face of all adversity and difficulties.

Using this word, and elaborating on each letter, I have been able to speak without notes for 60 or 90 minutes and never lose my place. The audience loves it and looks forward eagerly to the meaning of each letter as I explain it.

You can use this method with a three-letter word or a 10-letter word. It is an effective way to organize your thoughts and impress your audience by speaking fluently without notes.

Put Your Points on Index Cards

If you are using a podium, one of the best preparation techniques is to put your key points onto three-by-five-inch or five-by-eight-inch index cards in large letters. Rather than writing out your material word for word, write out key sentences, ideas, and phrases, and then shuffle the index cards from one to the next as you speak.

I have seen quite competent and highly respected speakers stand in front of a large audience with several index cards in their hands, using them as props as they give their talk to the audience. The audience seldom objects to this method of presentation. They all know that this is how the speaker is keeping his thoughts organized. They also recognize that the speaker has done considerable preparation to reach this point.

Give Your Talk to Small Groups First

One way that you can prepare is to give your talk to smaller, friendlier groups as many times as possible before you get in front of a larger, less personal audience. Not long ago, I attended a board meeting that was to be followed by a major dinner. One of the board members began speaking extemporaneously about a particular subject. Because he was so well organized, the entire board listened to him as he spoke and developed his theme, point by point, for 20 minutes. At the end, everybody was impressed with his thoughts and ideas.

That evening, in front of 500 people at the dinner, he stood up and gave the identical speech he had given at the boardroom table. I only realized in retrospect that the board meeting had been his final dry run for what turned out to be a very important and consequential talk to a large group of important people.

Walk and Talk

One way many people prepare for a speech is to go for a walk and give the talk as they go. As they walk along, they use their hands and faces and develop the talk. They use a mnemonic so they can remember every part without notes. Some even raise their voices on certain points and pretend that they are speaking loudly to people in a large audience. Walking and talking is one of the most effective ways to prepare for a speech.

Google the Information You Need

When you are speaking to a specific industry group, it is important that you at least appear well informed, if not an expert. You can achieve this by using Google to find all the information available on that industry. You can also go to Hoovers.com and look up industry statistics and trends, the major players in an industry, and the major events taking place in that industry group.

When you weave this "inside information" into your talk to a specific group, you sound like an insider. You sound like someone who works in the industry, if not somewhere in the company. People are greatly impressed by a speaker who seems to know a lot about what they do for a living and the challenges they are facing in the current marketplace.

Research the Key People

Finally, one of your best forms of preparation is to find out about the key people in the organization that has asked you to speak. Look up their biographies on the Internet. If a key person works for a corporation, her biography is often on the company website. Sometimes, you can ask the meeting planners for background information on the key people who are in the audience.

When I speak to a group, I make it a point to learn the names and backgrounds of the key people, and then I weave their names into my talk as I go along. I will say something like, "You've probably heard Ralph Wilson make this point many times—that you have to persist in the face of all adversity. That's the sort of thing that he believes and that's the reason for the success of this organization."

I can confidently say that I have never been contradicted afterward. When you put positive words, thoughts, and ideas into the mouths of the key people in your audience, they will always be flattered and happy as a result, and you will look like a hero.

Summary

People often ask me what the secret is to effective public speaking. I always tell them that it starts with preparation. Fully 90 percent of your success as a speaker will be determined by how well and how thoroughly you prepare. Within a few minutes of opening your mouth, the audience will know how well you have prepared and either grade you up or grade you down. Your job is to prepare and overprepare so that you sound like an authority from the first moment you begin to speak.

The best news is that the more you plan and prepare, the more confidence you will have when you finally stand up to speak. When you have practiced your talk over and over again, you will feel a tremendous sense of personal power and calmness when you finally stand before an audience.

CHAPTER 3

Self-Confidence and Mental Mastery

Eliminating the Fear of Public Speaking

Think positively and masterfully, with confidence and faith, and life becomes more secure, more fraught with action, richer in experience and achievement.

—EDDIE RICKENBACKER

Your goal when you speak is to stand up confidently: positive, relaxed, and feeling wonderful about yourself. Your ideal is to feel happy to be there, just as you would feel at a family Christmas party.

Here's the question: How do you achieve this state of calmness, clarity, and confidence in front of any audience? This is what you will learn in this chapter.

First, realize that stage fright is normal and natural, even for professionals who have appeared on the stage thousands of times. David Niven, the British actor, admitted that after thousands of performances he still threw up every single time before he went on stage.

According to the *Book of Lists*, 54 percent of adults rate fear of public speaking ahead of the fear of death. But as they say, there is nothing wrong with having butterflies in your stomach. Your goal is to get them to fly in formation.

All Fears Are Learned

The good news is that children are born with no fears at all. All fears that you have as an adult are the result of childhood experiences and negative reinforcement, both from others and from yourself. Because these fears, including the fear of speaking in front of an audience, have been learned, they can be unlearned as well.

The primary cause of adult fears is destructive criticism in childhood. When parents destructively criticize a child for any reason, he or she soon develops fears of failure and rejection. The fear of rejection or criticism leads to hypersensitivity to the opinions of others later in life.

Psychologists also say that almost all mental and emotional problems stem back to "love withheld" as a child. This happens when the parent, in an attempt to manipulate and control the child, gives or withholds love as a tool to influence the child's behavior. As a result, the child soon thinks, "As long as I do what

Mommy or Daddy wants, I'm safe. If I don't do what they approve of, I'm not safe."

Sensitive Children, Hypersensitive Adults

A child who is subjected to destructive criticism or love withheld becomes an adult who is overly concerned with the opinions of other people and their attitudes toward him. In extreme cases, the person can become so afraid and insecure that he cannot do anything until he is sure the key people in his life approve.

Many people are traumatized by the very idea of standing up and speaking in front of others. This is a manifestation of the fears of failure and rejection instilled prior to the age of five. But these feelings can be replaced with feelings of confidence, calmness, competence, and self-control.

Many of today's top speakers were so nervous at one time that they trembled at the very thought of speaking in front of others, even in staff meetings. A friend of mine, who speaks confidently to thousands of people today, wet his pants and had to run off the stage at his first public talk.

Start with Your Message

Confident public speaking begins with having a message that you really want people to hear. This is extremely important.

When someone tells me that he or she wants to be a better speaker, my first question is, "Why?" What is it that this person feels so strongly about that she wants to share her ideas with others?

Alas, in many cases, people want to be successful speakers so they can earn a lot of money, or gain the praise and acclaim of

others. They have given little or no thought to their subjects. In
my experience, these people seldom ever rise above mediocrity.
But if you have a subject that you feel strongly about and want
to share with others, you will find a way to become effective in
expressing yourself.

Speak from the Heart

Some years ago I heard Wally Amos, the founder of Famous Amos
Cookies, give a talk on combating adult illiteracy. He was dedicat-
ing a good deal of his time and money to helping adults learn how
to read. When he spoke to the 600 adults in the audience, he spoke
from his heart. He obviously had no particular training as a
speaker, but he had organized his thoughts and ideas in a logical
sequence. He spoke with great sincerity about the importance of
adults learning how to read and how it could change their lives. At
the end of his talk, he got a standing ovation from the entire room.
He was speaking from his heart on a subject he understood and
cared about.

The Audience Is on Your Side

The starting point of overcoming your fears or nervousness in
public speaking is to realize that when you stand up to speak,
everyone in the audience wants you to succeed. It is very much
like going to a movie. Have you ever gone to a movie hoping that
it would be a bad movie and a waste of time? Of course not! When
you go to a movie, you are wishing and hoping that it will be a
good movie and that it will justify the time and expense you have
invested. It is the same when you give a talk. The audience members are pulling for you. They all want you to succeed, exactly as if

they were attending a prize ceremony for you. They are there to cheer you on. They are eagerly wishing and hoping that your talk will be successful and enjoyable.

To put it another way, when you stand up to speak, you start with an *A*. You already have a top grade. Your job is merely to keep your *A* in the course of your remarks. Remember the Toastmasters process of systematic desensitization. By standing up and speaking over and over again, you will eventually lose most of your fear and trepidation. There is nothing that is more helpful in developing confidence than repetition.

How to Build Confidence and Competence

There are several specific techniques you can use to overcome fear and anxiety when you speak. The best speakers in the world use these methods continually.

Verbalize

Fully 95 percent of your emotions are determined by what you tell yourself. That is, your self-talk largely controls how you think, feel, and act. And you have complete control over the words that are flowing through your conscious mind.

The most powerful words that you can use to prepare yourself mentally for a speech, or for any event, are the words *I like myself*!

Before you get up to speak, say to yourself over and over, "I like myself! I like myself! I like myself!" These words have a wonderful effect in raising your self-esteem and lowering your fears. The more you like yourself, the more confident you will become. The more you like yourself, the more relaxed you will be. The more you like yourself, the more you will like the people you are speaking to. And the more you like yourself, the better you will perform when you get up to speak.

When you are feeling nervous or afraid for any reason, you can short-circuit these fears by repeating, "I can do it! I can do it! I can do it!" The fears of failure and rejection are expressed in the notion "I can't! I can't! I can't!" When you say the words *I can do it*, you cancel out the negative message and short-circuit the fear. When you try this for the first time, you will be amazed at how much better you feel and how much more confidently you speak.

Visualize

All improvement in your outer performance begins with an improvement in your mental pictures. When you create a clear, positive, exciting mental image of yourself speaking effectively, your subconscious mind accepts this as a command and then gives you the words, feelings, and gestures that are consistent with your mental picture.

You should "see" yourself standing calm, confident, relaxed, and smiling as you address your audience. See the audience leaning toward you, smiling, laughing, enjoying, and hanging on every word you say, as if you were amazingly intelligent and entertaining. Here are two visualization techniques you can use.

Internal and External Visualization.

With external visualization, you imagine yourself up on the stage as though you were a third party or an audience member looking on. You see yourself standing there calmly, confident and erect, totally relaxed, and fluent in your subject. You see yourself as someone else watching you sees you speak to the group. With internal visualization, you see yourself and your audience through your own eyes. You imagine the audience around you responding to you in a positive way.

You can alternate back and forth, seeing yourself from the inside and then seeing yourself from the outside, both in a positive way. This impresses your subconscious mind with a picture of you performing at your very best. Your subconscious mind will then respond by giving you the thoughts and feelings consistent with your picture.

Programming Your Mind

Another way to develop confidence and calmness in public speaking is to visualize yourself giving your talk in an excellent fashion, especially before you fall asleep. Your subconscious mind is more amenable to reprogramming in the last few minutes before you doze off and in the first few minutes after you wake up than at any other time in the day.

When you are falling asleep, visualize yourself giving a wonderful talk to an upcoming audience. This last impression soaks into your subconscious mind and affects you at a deep level while you sleep. The more often you repeat this exercise, the more calm and confident you will be when it actually comes time for you to speak to your audience. This method of mental rehearsal is very powerful.

Emotionalize

You can actually "get the feeling" that you would like to have if you were already a successful and popular speaker. In other words, you can manufacture the emotions of happiness, joy, pride, excitement, and confidence by creating these feelings in yourself prior to speaking. You do this by imagining that you have just given a wonderful talk and everyone is standing, smiling, cheering, and clapping. You then imagine feeling wonderful about yourself and the great job that you have just done.

When you are by yourself, create these feelings exactly as they would exist if your talk was as successful as you desire. Generate these feelings, and combine them with the statement "I give a wonderful talk every time." Combine these feelings with the visual picture you have of yourself as a fluent and competent professional speaker.

Famous psychologist and philosopher William James once said, "The very best way to achieve a feeling is to act as if you already had that feeling." The actions are much more under the control of the will than the feelings. If you act as if you already had a feeling, you actually trigger that feeling. This is the key to successful acting and stage performances of all kinds.

One good emotionalizing technique is called the "End-of-the-Movie" method. To understand this method, imagine that you arrive at your local theater to see a movie. But you are early, and the previous showing of the movie you have come to see is not quite finished. Nonetheless, you go in and watch the last 10 minutes of the movie. You see how the drama resolves itself and how everything works out well for everyone in the end.

When the movie lets out, you go back to the lobby for a few minutes until the movie starts again. You then go back into the theater and watch it from the beginning. Only this time, you already know how it ends. You know that the movie ends well, with the twists and turns of the plot all resolved successfully. As a result of knowing the end, you are much more relaxed as the plot unfolds. You enjoy the various scenes without becoming emotional, because you know it ends well.

In the same way, use the "End-of-the-Movie" technique for each speech you give. Imagine that you have reached the end of your talk and everyone is smiling and applauding. You have done a wonderful job. You feel happy, proud, and excited. Your friends in the audience are smiling with appreciation and pleasure. You imagine the end of your speech before you even begin to give it.

You can practice this method alone, over and over, before you speak. You will be amazed at how often your speech will end exactly as you visualized it.

Actualize

Here is an important discovery: Your subconscious mind cannot tell the difference between a real event and an event that you vividly imagine. For example, if you have an actual success experience, your subconscious mind records that as *one* success experience. This remembered success experience will give you greater confidence in the next similar experience, especially in speaking.

However, if you visualize, emotionalize, and imagine a successful experience, even if you have not had it yet, as far as your subconscious mind is concerned, you are actually having that experience in the outside world. So if you visualize and replay a positive speaking experience 10 or 20 or 50 times in your mind, your subconscious mind records that you have just given 10 or 20 or 50 successful talks, all ending in standing ovations and happy audiences.

When you practice this method, repeating your mental picture of success over and over, your subconscious mind finally becomes so convinced that you are excellent at speaking that you just naturally feel the calmness, clarity, and confidence that go along with being a complete professional.

When you bring the three together—verbalization, visualization, and emotionalization—you actually program your subconscious mind for success and prepare yourself to speak well in front of any audience.

Last-Minute Confidence Builders

Much of the mental preparation for public speaking can be done far in advance. But there are a few things speakers can do to calm their nerves immediately before speaking and thereby improve their performances.

Check Out the Room

When it is time for you to give your speech, arrive early and check out the room completely. Go up on the stage and stand behind the lectern. Walk around the room so that you can see where you will be speaking from the point of view of the audience.

Speak to some of the early arrivals, and ask them questions about where they are from and what they do. Ask for their names and give them your name. The more you talk to different audience participants before you stand up to speak, the more relaxed you will be. You will feel as if you are among friends.

When you are introduced and you begin speaking, seek out the people in the audience whom you spoke to earlier and look at them directly, smiling, as though this were a one-to-one conversation with an old friend. This will cause you to relax and feel in calm control of your material.

Do Some Breathing Exercises for Relaxation

Immediately prior to speaking, you can relax yourself and prepare to give an excellent talk by breathing deeply several times. The best formula for deep breathing is what I call the "7 x 7 x 7" method. What you do is to breathe in deeply—as deeply as possible—to the slow count of seven. You then hold your breath to the count of seven, and then exhale slowly to the count of seven.

You repeat this breathing exercise seven times, breathing in, holding your breath, and letting it out slowly. When you breathe deeply and hold it, you briefly drop into the alpha level of mind, clear your thinking, calm your nerves, and prepare yourself to speak well.

Pump Yourself Up

Just before you are introduced, say to yourself, "This is a great talk! I can hardly wait! This is going to be a great speech!" Repeat to yourself, "I like myself! I like myself! I like myself!"

Say these words with emotion, like you are trying to convince someone on the other side of the room that you really believe the words. The more emotionally you speak to yourself, the greater the positive impact it has on your subconscious and on your behavior.

Wiggle Your Toes

One way to increase your confidence and lower your fears is to wiggle your toes just before you go up to speak. As it happens, when you are really happy and excited, especially as a child, you wiggle your toes. When you wiggle your toes before you speak, it makes you more positive and enthusiastic. It actually makes you smile and feel happy. Remember, the actions create the feelings just as the feelings create the actions.

Roll Your Shoulders

Because much of a person's tension centers in the back and shoulders before a speech, you can relax yourself by rolling your shoulders several times. Shake your hands loosely, as if you were trying to shake water off of your fingers. This act seems to relieve tension and stress as well. When you combine them all—deep breathing, shoulder rolling, hand shaking, and toe wiggling—you'll feel relaxed, happy, and ready to speak.

Stand Erect

When you stand up to speak, hold your head up straight and erect. Imagine that there is a string running from the top of your head to the ceiling and that you are dangling from the string. Thinking of a string holding your head erect actually makes you stand up straighter and gives your entire bearing an attitude of confidence and power.

Think About Your Audience

Find a way to put yourself in a position of power over the audience mentally. For example, before you begin speaking, imagine that the audience is made up of people who owe you money. They have all come here to ask you to give them more time to pay.

You can also imagine that the audience members are sitting there in their underwear. This mental picture makes you smile to yourself, reduces tension, and makes your talk more effective.

When you think about your audience members like this, you become far more relaxed when speaking to them.

Be Grateful

A great way to increase your confidence with an audience is to practice gratitude for having this opportunity to speak. Say to yourself, "I am so grateful that I have a chance to speak to these people. Thank you! Thank you! Thank you!" Imagine that you really care about the audience. Say over and over to yourself, "I love my audience! I love my audience! I love my audience!"

Professional speakers are familiar with the expression "the privilege of the platform." When you stand up to speak, always think of the wonderful privilege you have to be able to share your ideas with these remarkable people. The more grateful you are for the opportunity to speak to them, the more positive and enthusiastic you will be with every word.

The more you genuinely like and care about the people you are speaking to, the more confident you will be. The more you see them as friends who like you, and whom you like in return, the more relaxed you will be.

It's Not About You

Finally, remember that it is not about you. It's about them. Get out of yourself and your personal concerns about what they may think of you. Instead, project into the minds of your audience mentally and emotionally and think exclusively about them.

My friend Cavett Robert, founder of the National Speakers Association and a wonderful man, once said that as a young speaker, he would rush onto the stage with the attitude of "Here I am!" He said that he only began to become an excellent speaker when he reversed his attitude. Instead of thinking "Here I am!" he would hurry onto the stage with the feeling of "Wow, there you are!"

When you begin to see your audience as a room full of wonderful, exceptional, warm, charming, and interesting people, you will have the same attitude of "Wow, there you are!" and your fears will diminish. You will become calm, confident, warm, friendly, and positive. You will be on your way to becoming one of the best speakers in your field.

Summary

Mental fitness is like physical fitness, based on a series of exercises, practiced over and over. When you apply these methods and techniques for calmness and mental mastery before you speak, you will soon feel calm, confident, and in complete control every time.

Start Strong with Any Audience

The beginning is the most important part of any work, especially in the case of a young and tender thing; for that is the time at which the character is being formed and the desired impression is more readily taken.

—PLATO

Y ou have heard the saying "First impressions are lasting; you never get a second chance to create a good first impression." I'm sure you've also heard this one: "Well begun is half done."

When you start your speech, you must focus everything on making a positive first impression on your audience members.

This opens them up and prepares them to listen to and be affected by your remarks.

Your Introduction

If you're making a presentation where someone is introducing you, it's the introduction that sets the stage. The purpose of the introduction is to build expectancy in the audience. Its goal is to cause the audience to lean forward mentally and emotionally to hear what you have to say. Therefore, you must carefully plan your introduction in advance.

A good introduction sets the stage by telling the audience about your accomplishments. It then leads to the title of your speech. Your name comes last. Depending on the topic or length of your talk, it can be brief or expanded.

Here is a short example: "Our speaker tonight has started 22 businesses and made more than one million dollars in eight different enterprises. Today he is going to tell us how we can 'Succeed in Business By Really Trying.' Please put your hands together and help me welcome Mr. Brian Tracy."

A longer introduction would include more details about the background and accomplishments of the speaker, especially as they relate to the subject. The focus is always on building expectancy and credibility so that the audience members have the attitude of "I can hardly wait to hear what this person has to say."

After the Introduction

Lots of things need to happen between the end of the introduction and the beginning of your speech, so keep the next five things in mind as you are taking the stage. They will help you make a posi-

tive impression on the audience and set the right tone for your speech.

Step up Confidently

When you are introduced, step up to the podium and shake hands with the introducer. Give him or her a hug if it is appropriate. Let the introducer leave the stage, and then turn to the audience.

Start with silence to settle and to center the audience. Smile and sweep your eyes slowly around the room for a few seconds, as if you are really happy to be there with these people.

As you stand silently, smiling, the audience will very quickly settle down, becoming silent and attentive, waiting for you to begin. When the tension is palpable and everyone is silent, begin with a strong, clear, friendly, interesting, attention-grabbing opening statement that leads into your talk and ties into your closing remarks.

Look the Part

The rule here is that nothing in your clothes or grooming should distract from you or your message. People make a decision about you in the first 30 seconds. For this reason, your image, your dress, grooming, and stance are very important.

Your appearance tells the audience how you think and feel about yourself. It is an expression of your own self-image. Your appearance also tells the audience members how you think and feel about them. The rule is, "If it doesn't help, it hurts."

Many speakers think that it is "cool" to get up in front of an audience dressed casually, as if they had just been working in the garden. But what this often tells the audience is that you respect neither yourself nor them. This impression downgrades the perceived value of what you have to say.

Time and time again, my clients hold their annual meetings in beautiful resorts in the South and West. They will say, "Everyone will be dressed country-club casual" and that I am welcome to dress casually as well. I never take them up on their offer. The rule is to always dress equal to or better than your audience. You must always look like a professional.

A friend of mine is a good young speaker. But he grew up in a poor home. As a result, he was not particularly knowledgeable about proper dress or choice of accessories. Someone had given him a large gold pinky ring for Christmas. He wore it on his small finger and waved it around as he spoke. He thought it was attractive.

On one occasion, after he gave a speech, the meeting organizer took him aside and said, "You are a good person, and you have a good message, but when you wear that pinky ring, you look like a pimp."

He had no idea he was making that impression. He took it off and never wore it again.

Build Positive Expectations

Your first job is to raise expectations. You want to make the audience members feel glad that they came. You want them to be open and eager to hear more.

Remember that everyone in your audience wants you to succeed. They are already on your side. They sincerely want your talk to be a good one. Your first words should confirm that it will be.

It is important that the audience like you from the start. The more likeable people perceive you to be, the more open the audience members will be to your message, and the less resistant they will be to any controversial points or ideas that you bring up.

Take Charge Immediately

When you stand up to speak, you become the leader. The people in the audience want you to be in control. They want you to take charge of the room. Act as if you own the room and as if everyone works for you. They will follow your commands.

When you are introduced, walk straight to where you will be speaking, shoulders up, smiling and confident, with your eyes wide open and your chin up. Be alert and aware and walk briskly, with energy and determination.

When you begin speaking, focus in on a single person in the audience. Start off by speaking directly and warmly to him or her. Then, casually move on to another face, and then another, and another. This direct eye contact slows you down, calms your nerves, and helps you to develop a relationship with the people in your audience.

Be Authentic and Humble

The very best way to be liked is to be both authentic and humble.

You achieve authenticity by being genuine and open. You can appear a little embarrassed and overwhelmed by the positive attention the audience is giving to you. Smile openly and warmly as your eyes sweep the audience.

You exude humility by not appearing as if you know it all or as if you are superior to the audience in any way. Sometimes, after I receive a glowing introduction, I will turn to the introducer and say, "Thank you. You read that exactly the way my wife wrote it. But I still can't get my kids to go to bed when I tell them."

A Long List of Ways to Start a Speech

Now that you're in the spotlight, how do you get the ball rolling? There are several ways that you can start a talk effectively. All of them are intended to engage your audience right off the bat so that you have everyone's full attention for the duration of your speech.

Thank the Organizers

You can start by thanking the audience for coming and thanking the organization for inviting you to speak. Refer to the person who introduced you or to one or more of the senior people in the organization in the audience. This compliments them, makes them feel proud and happy about your presence, and connects you into the audience like an electrical plug in a socket.

Start with a Positive Statement

You can begin by telling the audience members how much they will like and enjoy what you have to say. For example, you might say: "You are really going to enjoy the time we spend together this evening. I am going to share with you some of the most important ideas that have ever been discovered in this area."

Compliment the Audience

You can begin by complimenting the audience members sincerely and with great respect. Smile as if you are really glad to see them, as if they are all old friends of yours that you have not seen for quite a while.

You can tell them that it is a great honor for you to be here, that they are some of the most important people in this business or industry, and that you are looking forward to sharing some key ideas with them. You could say something like, "It is an honor to be here with you today. You are the elite, the top 10 percent of people in this industry. Only the very best people in any field will take the time and make the sacrifice to come so far for a conference like this."

Make a Thought-Provoking Statement About the Audience

Often when I am speaking to the members of an entrepreneurial or networking group, I will start off with, "Thank you very much for having me. I was just told that today I would be addressing a roomful of self-made millionaires."

After making this statement, I stand silently, smiling and looking around, allowing my words to soak in. I then continue by saying, "What I learned was that everyone here is either a self-made millionaire or intends to be sometime in the future. Is that correct?"

This opening always brings a loud chorus of "Yes!" Everyone smiles and agrees that his or her goal is to be a self-made millionaire. After this kind of opening, everyone is wide-awake, alert, and ready to hear what else I have to say.

Refer to Current Events

Use a current front-page news story to transition into your subject and to illustrate or prove your point. You can bring a copy of the newspaper and hold it up as you refer to it in your introduction. This visual image of you holding the paper and reciting or reading a key point rivets the audience's attention and causes people to learn forward to hear what you have to say.

Refer to a Historical Event

For many years, I studied military history. Especially, I studied the lives and campaigns of the great generals and the decisive battles they won. One of my favorites was Alexander the Great.

One day, I was asked to give a talk on leadership principles to a roomful of managers for a Fortune 500 company. I decided that the campaign of Alexander the Great against Darius of Persia would make an excellent story that would illustrate the leadership qualities of one of the great commanders in history. I opened my talk with these words:

> Once upon a time there was a young man named Alex who grew up in a poor country. But Alex was a little bit ambitious. From an early age, he decided that he wanted to conquer the entire known world. But there was a small problem. Most of the known world was under the control of a huge multinational called the Persian Empire, headed by King Darius II. To fulfill his ambition, Alex was going to have to take market share away from the market leader, who was very determined to hold on to it.
>
> This is the same situation that exists between you and your major competitors in the market today. You are going to have to use all your leadership skills to win the great marketing battles of the future.

Refer to a Well-Known Person

You can start by quoting a well-known person or publication that recently made an important statement. Here's an example:

> Today we are going to talk about why it is that some people earn more money than others. Gary Becker, the Nobel Prize–winning economist, wrote recently that almost all income inequality in America is the result of a knowledge and skills gap. In the next few minutes, I am going to show you how you can develop the knowledge and skills you need to narrow this gap and lead your field in the years ahead.

Here's another example: One of the subjects I touch upon regularly is the importance of continual personal and professional development. I will say something like, "In the twenty-first century, knowledge and know-how are the keys to success. As basketball coach Pat Riley said, 'If you are not getting better, you are getting worse.'"

Repeat a Recent Conversation

Start by telling a story about a recent conversation with someone in attendance. For instance, I might say, "A few minutes ago, I was talking with Tom Robinson in the lobby. He told me that this is one of the very best times to be working in this industry, and I agree."

Make a Shocking Statement

You can start your talk by making a shocking statement of some kind. For example, you might say something like, "According to a recent study, there will be more change, more competition, and more opportunities in this industry in the next year than ever before. And 72 percent of the people in this room will be doing something different within two years if they do not rapidly adapt to these changes."

Quote from Recent Research

You can start by quoting from a recent research report. One example is, "According to a story in a recent issue of *Business Week*, there were almost 9,000,000 millionaires in America in 2007, most of them self-made. And this number is going to double by the year 2015."

Give Them Hope

The French philosopher Gustav Le Bon once wrote, "The only religion of mankind is, and has always been, hope."

When you speak effectively, you give people hope of some kind. Remember, the ultimate purpose of speaking is to inspire a change of thought, feeling, and action. It is to motivate and inspire people to do things that they would not have done in the absence of your comments. Everything you say should relate to the actions you want people to take and the reasons that they should take those actions.

Start with Humor—Maybe

You can start a talk with humor, but only if you are naturally funny. You must be sure that the audience will interpret your story or joke as humorous. For this reason, you should try out your humor several times on other people to make sure that it works well. Only use humor if you personally think that the joke or story is funny, you can deliver it well, and the audience is likely to be receptive.

Some of the best professional speakers start with humor that is so pointed and appropriate that it cracks up the audience members and grabs their complete attention. But this is an art. It takes a special type of personality to use humor effectively.

Here is an important point. It is fairly easy to start with a joke of some kind. I used to do this to open almost every talk. Then I learned that my initial remarks set the tone for what is to come. If I start with humor, the audience assumes that my talk is going to be funny and entertaining. If I then switch into a more serious or thoughtful subject, people will often become confused and disappointed. Be careful.

Be an Entertainer

Bill Gove, one of the best speakers in America, would walk onto the stage after his introduction as if he had just finished talking to someone on the side and was breaking off to give his talk to the group. The audience got the feeling that his entire talk was one continuous conversation.

Bill would often go to the edge of the stage and then drop his voice in a conspiratorial way, open his arms, and beckon the audience members to come a little closer. He would say, "Come here, let me tell you something," and then he would wave them forward as though he was about to tell a secret to the entire room.

The amazing thing was that everyone in the room would lean forward to hear this "secret" that he was about to share. People would all suddenly realize what they were doing and break out in laughter. It was a wonderful device to get the audience into the palm of his hands.

Ask a Question, Conduct a Survey

You can open by making a positive statement and then asking a question requiring a show of hands. Try something like this: "This is a great time to be alive and in business in America. By the way, how many people here are self-employed?"

Raise your hand to indicate what you want people to do. I have used this line, and after a number of hands go up, I then say to someone who raised her hand in the front, "How many people here are *really* self-employed?"

Invariably, someone will say, "We all are!"

I then compliment and affirm the answer: "You're right! We are all self-employed, from the time we take our first jobs to the day we retire; we all work for ourselves, no matter who signs our paychecks."

Get Them Talking to One Another

You can ask people to turn to the person next to them to discuss a particular point. For instance, you could say, "Tell the person next to you what you would like to learn from this seminar."

Whatever you ask your audience members to do, within reason, they will do it for you. Your commands and your leadership will easily influence them, as long as you ask them with confidence.

Open with a Problem

You can start with a problem that must be solved. If it is a problem that almost everyone has in common, you will immediately have the audience's complete and undivided attention. For example, you could say:

> Fully 63 percent of baby boomers are moving toward retirement without enough money put aside to provide for themselves for as long as they are going to live. We must address this problem and take action immediately to ensure that each person who retires will be able to live comfortably for the rest of his or her natural life.

Make a Statement, Ask a Question

You can start by making a strong statement and then asking a question. You then follow with an answer and ask another question. This gets people immediately involved and listening to your every word. Here's an example:

> Twenty percent of the people in our society make 80 percent of the money. Are you a member of the top 20 percent? If not, would you like to join the top 20 percent or even the top 10 percent? Well, in

the next few minutes, I am going to give you some ideas to help you become some of the highest-paid people in our society. Would that be a good goal for our time together today?

It is an interesting psychological phenomenon that people are conditioned from infancy to respond when they are asked a question. Whenever you ask a question of any kind, people instinctively and automatically answer you, even if only to themselves.

When you ask, "How many people here would like to double their incomes in the next one to two years?" almost all of the audience members will instinctively and automatically raise their hands or shout out agreement.

Whenever you ask a question and then pause a few seconds to allow people to process the question, you take complete control of the audience. The fact is that the person who asks the questions controls the conversation and controls the person who is answering the question.

Even if people do not answer aloud, they are helpless to stop themselves from answering. Sometimes I demonstrate this point by asking some common questions such as, "What color is your car?"

Everyone in the audience automatically *thinks* about the answer. I ask, "What is your address?" People automatically and instinctively *think* of their addresses. People cannot *not* answer when they are asked questions.

Start with a Story

You can start your talk with a story. Some of the most powerful words to grab the complete attention of the audience are "Once upon a time . . ."

From infancy and early childhood, people love stories of any kind. When you start off with the words "Once upon a time . . ." you tell the audience that a story is coming. People immediately settle down, become quiet, and lean forward like kids around a campfire. When I conduct full-day seminars and I want to bring people back to their seats after a break, I will say loudly, "Once upon a time there was a man, right here in this city . . ."

As soon as I say these words, people hurry back to their seats and begin to listen attentively to the rest of the story.

Build a Bridge

One of the most important parts of starting a speech is to build a bridge between yourself and the audience members. Begin with something that you and the audience have in common. It can be the fact that you work today, or have worked in the past, in their industry. You may have children, just as they do. You could be familiar with their town or a supporter of the local football or basketball team. You could even have a concern or problem that is similar to the concerns and problems that the members of the audience are facing in their lives or work.

When you take a few minutes to build a bridge of commonality between yourself and the audience members, you immediately put them on your side. They see you as "one of them." They become more open to your words and comments. They become more forgiving of any mistakes you make. They feel that you are more knowledgeable and approachable because of your common backgrounds.

Tell Them About Yourself

Very often, I will start a speech to a business, sales, or entrepreneurial group by saying, "I started off without graduating from high school. My family had no money. Everything I accomplished in life I had to do on my own with very little help from anyone else."

It is amazing how many people come up to me after a talk that began with those words and tell me that was their experience as well. They tell me that they could immediately identify with me because they too had started with poor grades and limited funds, as most people do. As a result they were open to the rest of my talk, even a full-day seminar, and felt that everything I said was more valid and authentic than if I had been a person who started off with a successful background. Building a bridge like this is very helpful in bringing the audience onto your side.

Summary

The ability to start strong with any audience is a learned skill. Knowing how to structure an introduction and knowing how to take the stage can make or break your speech. And by finding ways to open your talk with greater warmth, friendliness, or impact, you can have the audience eating out of the palm of your hand within 30 seconds of beginning to speak. This is your goal.

CHAPTER 5

Mastering Meetings with Small Groups

The effective man always states at the outset of a meeting the specific purpose and contribution it is to achieve. He always, at the end of his meetings, goes back to the opening statement and relates the final conclusions to the original intent.

—PETER DRUCKER

Your ability to speak well and persuasively in small meetings can have an extraordinary impact on your life and career.

In business, others continually assess and evaluate you. Consciously and subconsciously, they are upgrading or downgrading their opinions of your personality, ability, competence, and level of confidence. For this reason, you must think of business meetings as important events in your career. You cannot allow a meeting with two or more people to unfold by chance, especially when fully 50 percent of management time is spent in meetings of some kind and most people feel that 50 percent of this time is wasted because of poor planning and organization.

Peter Drucker once wrote, "The meeting is an essential tool of the executive." An executive is defined as anyone who is responsible for results. According to this definition, virtually everyone is an executive of some kind, including yourself.

Small-Group Meetings Are Important

Many of your presentations and speaking engagements will be with smaller groups of people, sometimes as few as one or two others. These meetings, just like a large talk or presentation, must be prepared for and planned with care. How you perform can make or break your career.

Some years ago, I was conducting a strategic-planning exercise with a large company. Executives were brought in from all over the country and from distant branches. At the meeting, several of the executives from the head office were clearly detached and uncaring about how the strategic-planning session unfolded. But there were two young executives from distant branches who were thoroughly prepared and active participants in every question brought up during the discussions.

At one of the breaks, I was doing a debrief with the president of the company about the progress of the meeting. He said to me, "Did you notice how important the contributions of those two guys have been to this meeting?" It was clear to everyone that these two executives were more prepared and involved than any of the others. He was obviously impressed.

About a month later, in the business section of the local news-paper, there was an announcement that both of these executives had been promoted to vice president. Some years later, one of those executives became the president of a billion-dollar com-pany. His contributions at the meeting as a young manager regis-tered with everyone and reverberated throughout his career.

A few months after that, the company also announced the "early retirements" of the senior executives from the head office who had sat there silently and contributed nothing to the meeting. Their careers in that company were finished.

Prepare Thoroughly

The starting point of meeting effectiveness is thorough prepara-tion. Preparation is immediately obvious to everyone who attends, as is the failure to prepare.

If you are running the meeting, plan it. Prepare an agenda. Select the people whom you are going to invite and inform them of their expected contributions. Organize the meeting as though it were an important part of your business life, because it is.

If you are an attendee at a meeting, plan your participation. Find out the purpose for the meeting and then be sure that you have something to contribute. Many people who attend business meetings sit quietly while the meeting goes on. But unfortunately, those who say nothing at a meeting are presumed to have nothing to say. This is not the kind of message you want to convey.

Consider the Importance of Seating

Arrive early at the meeting so that you can choose your seat with care. If it is your meeting, sit with your back to a wall, facing the entrance so that you have visual command of the room and you can see everyone entering and leaving. When I hold meetings, especially if they are important, I specifically designate where each person is going to sit in the meeting. This ensures that I have the most important people sitting in the most important places.

If it is someone else's meeting, select a place where you can sit facing the door and either kitty-corner or directly opposite the meeting leader. If you are not sure, ask the meeting leader where he or she would like you to sit. But you still have some control, and you should use it to your best advantage. Don't be afraid to ask if you can sit in a particular place or if you can change seats with someone else so that you have your back to a wall, or where you have greater eye contact with the key person in the meeting. This is essential to making your most valuable contribution and to being the most persuasive.

Be Punctual

Start on time. Assume that the latecomer is not coming, and begin. Thank the participants for coming and give the reason for the meeting. Explain the structure of the meeting and how it will be conducted. Give the end time for the meeting so that everyone knows when it will be over.

Types of Meetings

There are four different types of business meetings. These include:

1. *Problem Solving.* The purpose of the meeting is to discuss a problem and agree on a solution.
2. *Information Sharing.* The purpose of the meeting is to share

new information, make announcements, and be sure that everyone is informed of changes and assignments.

3. *New-Product Announcements.* The purpose of the meeting is to familiarize all the participants with new products and services that the company is offering or thinking about offering.

4. *Team Building.* The purpose of the meeting is to bring people together to talk about what they are doing and the progress they are making. Team-building meetings are powerful forms of developing the esprit de corps that is essential to a company.

The Meeting Leader

If you are leading the meeting, you should be thoroughly prepared with handouts to inform and illustrate to the participants the points you want to cover. If you are using PowerPoint or flip charts, you should prepare and practice with them thoroughly in advance. Be sure that you have everything that you need to conduct the meeting smoothly and professionally.

With your meeting agenda, start with the most important items first. This ensures that if you run out of time because of extended discussions you will have covered the 20 percent of items that account for 80 percent of the value.

The Active Participant

If you are a meeting participant, make a point of asking a question, making a statement, or taking a position within the first five minutes. People who speak up in the first five minutes take on a more dominant and significant role in the meeting in the eyes of other participants. People who fail to speak up until much later are often ignored or not considered to be of particular importance.

The goal of any meeting, to a large group or to a small group, is action of some kind. As the group discusses each item, you or someone else should be asking or insisting upon the action or actions that are going to take place as a result of this discussion and agreement.

Volunteer for Responsibilities

One way to be an active participant is to offer to do what needs doing. In every organization and on every team, 20 percent of the people do 80 percent of the work. The participants who ask for action and continually volunteer for more responsibility are seen by everyone as the most important and significant members of the team.

When a subject has been discussed, you should ask, "What is our action plan for this item? What do we do next?" Raise your hand and volunteer to accept responsibility for action on various items. The more you volunteer, the more valuable you will appear to the most important people in the meeting.

Prepare in Advance

When you are expected to contribute specific information at a meeting, you can always use the PREP Formula. Begin by stating your point of view, give your reasons for holding this point of view, follow up with an example of why your reasoning is correct, and then restate your point of view to round off your contribution. This is an extremely effective way of impressing the meeting planners and participants with your level of preparation.

Persuading Others

The key to success in a meeting is for you to be persuasive. It lets you affect the direction of the discussion and influence the final decisions and conclusions with your input.

To be persuasive in a meeting, the meeting participants must like you. To be liked, you must be *likeable*. People must willingly support you and approve of your ideas and your positions. The key to increasing your influence and persuading others to support and agree with you is simple: *Make others feel important.*

There are six things ("the six *As*") you can practice to make others feel more valuable in a meeting or any other social or business situation. They are essential if you want to speak to win.

1. *Acceptance.* One of the deepest human needs is to be unconditionally accepted by others. You express your acceptance of others by looking directly at them and smiling, both when they come in and when they say something or contribute to the meeting. This makes the individual feel valuable and important. It raises his or her self-esteem and improves his or her self-image. It also causes the person, at a subconscious level, to want to support you in the things you suggest or say.

2. *Appreciation.* Any time that you express appreciation to other people for anything that they have done or said, you raise their self-esteem and increase your likeability in their eyes. The easiest way to express appreciation is simply to say thank you for anything that the person does or says that is helpful or constructive. You can thank people for arriving on time. You can thank people for contributing a piece of information. You can thank people for making a comment and for assisting or correcting you.

Whenever you thank someone for anything, you encourage that person to repeat the behavior and to make even more valuable contributions. When a person is thanked, he feels more valuable, respected, and important. The words *thank you* are powerful in building your likeability and ensuring that others cooperate with you and support your positions.

3. *Admiration.* Abraham Lincoln once said, "Everyone likes a compliment." When you compliment people on anything that they do or say, or on any of their possessions, they feel more valuable and important, and they like you more as a result.

Continually look for ways to compliment people. You can admire a person's briefcase, purse, or pen. You can admire an item of his clothing or appearance. If he presents a piece of information, you can compliment him on how excellent it looks or sounds. Even looking at a person, smiling, and nodding in a complimentary way can cause him to feel more valuable and important and to like and support you when you propose something later.

4. *Approval.* You may have heard the saying "Babies cry for it and grown men die for it." People need approval from others, especially people whom they look up to and respect. Every time you give praise and approval of any kind to anyone for any reason, you raise that person's self-esteem, improve her self-image, and make her feel better about herself and about you.

The keys to giving approval are to make it both immediate and specific. When someone contributes something of value or presents a piece of helpful information to the group, immediately praise the information by saying something like, "This is very good work." Be specific. Say something like, "These figures are very impressive. They look great."

The more that you praise and approve the work and contributions of other people, the more and better contributions they will make, and the more they will like you and support your ideas and points of view later.

5. *Attention.* People always pay attention to people and things

that they most value. As the saying goes, life is the study of attention. Whenever you pay close attention to another person, he or she feels more valuable and important. The key to paying attention is to listen closely when another person speaks and not to interrupt. Look at the person directly and hang on every word. Nod, smile, and agree as if what the other person is saying is extraordinarily important and insightful.

When others feel that they are being closely listened to, their self-esteem goes up. Their brains release endorphins, and they feel happier and more positive about themselves and their work. They associate you with this good feeling, and your influence over them goes up tremendously.

6. *Agreement.* The final *A* that you can practice in any meeting with any number of people is to be generally agreeable with others. You can be agreeable even if you disagree with someone's point of view.

When someone says something or makes a point that you don't agree with, instead of challenging him (which puts him on the defensive and makes him angry) say something like, "That is an interesting point. I had not thought of that before. It clashes a bit with my own idea, but I would like to understand it better."

If you must disagree, use what is called "Third-Party Disagreement." Instead of saying, "I disagree with you," you can say, "That is an interesting point. How would you answer the question that another person might ask if he or she were to challenge this point by saying such and such a thing?"

In other words, put your disagreement into the mouth of a nonexistent third party. Ask the person to defend his point of view to a person who is not present. This takes the pressure off of the individual and it enables him to defend his point of view without having to feel defensive or under attack by anyone in that particular meeting.

Avoid Criticism or Negativity

If you are leading a meeting, you have tremendous power. Everyone looks up to and defers to you as the leader. Everything you say is magnified and multiplied, either in a positive or negative way.

When other people are contributing to the meeting, you should nod, smile, and support them. When someone is in a meeting with others, he is on the stage when he speaks. Any comment from anyone in the room, especially from a person senior to him, puts him under a spotlight. It can either make him feel valuable and important or make him feel vulnerable and defensive. Be careful about what you say.

Even a small criticism, a raise of the eyebrow, or a disgruntled look directed at a meeting participant is observed by everyone, and it makes the meeting participant feel diminished and insecure. You must use your position as the meeting leader with tremendous care, maintaining the self-esteem and self-respect of each meeting participant, irrespective of how you might feel about his or her ideas and comments.

If you are not happy about something another person does or says, remain calm and positive in front of the others and take the situation "off line." Arrange to meet with the person privately. The rule is to praise in public, appraise in private.

Avoid Barriers to Communication

When you sit opposite a person—across a table or desk, for example—the furniture can act as a physical and psychological barrier to communication. It subconsciously suggests that you are on op-posite sides and that your points of view are antagonistic.

To resolve this dilemma, one of the best things you can do is to ask to sit kitty-corner to the key person. When you sit next to a person rather than opposite him, unseen psychological barriers seem to drop and you communicate with greater warmth and friendliness. Don't be afraid to make it clear that you would prefer not to sit opposite the person but would prefer to sit next to him or her, where you can have direct eye contact.

In all my years, I have never had the person opposite me resist or refuse this request. In most cases, he had not thought of it him-self and was happy that I brought it up.

Summary

The mark of the professional in every field is preparation. The more thoroughly you prepare for a meeting of any kind, even with just one other person, the more effective you will appear and the better results you will get.

The power is always on the side of the person who has pre-pared the most thoroughly. The individual who comes into a meeting unprepared has diminished power and sometimes no power at all.

Your job is to speak to win on every occasion. Your goal is to be seen as an important player in every conversation. Your aim is to persuade others to your point of view and to make an impact on your world. You do this by thoroughly preparing for every meeting that you hold or that you participate in, and you do it by using techniques that make others feel important.

CHAPTER 6

Mastering Small-Group Presentations and Negotiations

The greatest good you can do for another is not just to share your own riches but to reveal to him his own.

—BENJAMIN DISRAELI

Most of the opportunities for you to win points speaking will take place in small business meetings. As I discussed in Chapter 5, it is important to know how to lead and participate in meetings effectively. But in these meetings, you will often be called upon to make a presentation of your point of view, product, or policy in an attempt to persuade others to agree with you and to support your recommended course of action.

So if business meetings are an essential tool for the executive, the presentations made in those meetings may be even more important. Many people have changed the entire direction of their careers, and their companies, by making an effective presentation to a small group of people with decision-making power. You can do the same.

Small-Group Presentations Can Make or Break Your Career

Each time you give a presentation to a small group, imagine that your future and your career hang in the balance. Imagine that this meeting is being videotaped to be shown to thousands of people. Imagine that there is a hidden camera on you while you are making your presentation and it is showing your presentation to people all over the country.

In other words, take the presentation seriously. The more seriously you take your presentation, in advance, the more seriously the participants will respond to you.

As in all meetings of any size, preparation is the key to success. It will account for fully 90 percent of the results that you get or fail to get. As a top lawyer once said to me, "I don't believe that there is any such word as *overprepare.*"

Start with the End in Mind

Determine your goals for the presentation. Idealize and ask yourself, "If this meeting were perfect, what would be the outcome?"

Think on paper. Write down the very best things that could possibly happen if your presentation were perfectly effective and you achieved every goal you had in mind. The greater clarity you have with regard to the perfect outcome, the easier it will be to prepare your presentation and the more likely it is that you will achieve those goals at the end.

Remember That Everything Is a Negotiation

When you are giving a small-group presentation in an attempt to persuade others to support you, you are engaging in a form of negotiation. Each person will come into the room with his own ideas and desires. Your aim is to bring the group around to your personal point of view and convince them to support your recommendations. This means that you will have to gradually change their minds, and in some cases, change their minds completely.

Think Like a Lawyer

Use the "Lawyer's Method" to prepare for a presentation. Lawyers learn to prepare the opponent's case before they prepare their own. To do this, write down everything that you think the other participants in the meeting will want or think that is in opposition to what you want to accomplish. If you can be specific, attach the particular objections and resistance to the particular people to whom you will be speaking.

Know the Difference Between Desire and Fear

With one group of executives at a large company with whom I negotiate once or twice a year, I begin by writing out the things I know about their concerns and reasons for skepticism or hesitancy. Most of all, I know that they are resistant to change. This is quite common when you are giving a presentation. People have a tendency to get into a comfort zone and then to resist any attempts or suggestions to move them out of this comfort zone.

The two primary motivations for buying—or for almost any other decision to change—are fear and desire. People are afraid of losing time, money, prestige, advantage, or something else. People desire more time, money, market share, opportunity, and so on.

Psychologists tell us that the motivating power of fear is two and a half times the motivating power of desire. This means that emphasizing what the participants can lose from not accepting your ideas is two and a half times more persuasive than emphasizing what they can gain. In many cases, however, the primary benefit you have to offer is that the participants will gain from your ideas. The main reason that anyone does anything revolves around the word *improvement.* That is, people take action because they believe that they will be better off as a result of acting than they would be if they did not act at all.

So even when you are appealing to fear—the fears of rejection, criticism, loss, embarrassment, disapproval, ridicule, and so on—you are suggesting that the participant's situation will improve relative to these fears if she takes your advice.

Understand the Meeting Participants

When making a presentation to a group of people, you are often dealing with several distinctly different personalities. This means that each person will have different fears and desires in different degrees of intensity. The more knowledgeable you are about what people want to accomplish and what they are afraid of experiencing, the easier it will be for you to tailor your remarks and address their concerns.

I know that the group of executives at the company I mentioned earlier has a strong resistance to change, but they also have a strong desire to increase their sales and profits. Therefore, I always focus on making a strong case for increased sales and profitability, and then, to allay their fears of loss, I suggest a low-cost, no-cost test of my idea to see if it is capable of delivering the proper revenues and profits that I am suggesting.

Over the years, I have found that people are usually quite open to a limited test with limited risk on a new idea. On the other hand, they are usually extremely tense about risking a large amount of money to try out an untested idea.

Understand Common Fears

Most adults are afraid of being manipulated or taken advantage of. They are afraid of being hustled; talked into doing something that is contrary to their short-term or long-term interests; being sold a product, service, or idea that they don't need, can't use, and can't afford; or of ending up worse off after they have accepted a recommendation than they were before.

People have these fears because, starting in childhood, they have been talked into doing or not doing things that have not turned out well and have been taken advantage of by a variety of people. As a result, they have an almost Pavlovian response to anyone who is attempting to persuade them to do anything. They are naturally skeptical and suspicious. Each time a person is taken advantage of and feels that he has come out on the short end of the stick, he says to himself consciously and subconsciously, "This won't happen to me again." You should consider this when making a small-group presentation.

Lower Their Resistance

Whenever you make a presentation for a new idea, product, or service, these fears are triggered in the minds and hearts of your listeners, making them naturally resistant and skeptical. Your job while speaking is to do everything possible to lower this resistance and remove this skepticism.

Use the Socratic method of presentation: When you want to introduce a new subject to another individual or group, always begin with the facts of the matter that everyone agrees with and around which there is no controversy. Then leverage these facts into areas that may be new and with which people may disagree.

Negotiating Big Deals

When I have negotiated large contracts with groups of people, often with myself on one side of the table and six to 10 other officials or executives on the other side of the table, I have always followed a strategy that has proved successful time after time.

We start off with a contract or a development agreement of 30, 40, or even 50 pages. I will have carefully reviewed every clause in the agreement ahead of time and will be quite clear about which clauses are most important to me and which elements of the contract are most important to the other parties. We then go through the agreement, paragraph by paragraph and line by line, discussing and agreeing or disagreeing with each point as we move along.

Eighty percent of the various clauses and subclauses in contracts are boilerplate and noncontroversial. We therefore go through all of these clauses, from the first to the last page, and agree on all of the things that we agree on. When we come to a part of the agreement where we disagree, I conduct a short discussion around this point to get the other side's thoughts and feelings, and then I say, "Why don't we put this point aside for now and come back to it later?" We then go on to the next point and continue to work step by step through the agreement, putting aside each controversial point as we go along so as not to interrupt the flow.

Once we have reviewed the entire agreement and agreed upon most of the clauses, we go back through the more controversial points. We discuss each point as thoroughly as possible. If one is a particularly emotional sticking point, I once again suggest that we put it aside.

The second time through the agreement, we will resolve about 80 percent of the 20 percent of unresolved issues, leaving us with about 4 percent of the total agreement left to be discussed and agreed upon.

By this time, we have agreement on as much as 96 percent of the clauses and subclauses. Everyone is positive and feeling a sense of forward progress. We can now go back through and discuss in depth, with less emotion and more openness, the unresolved parts of the contract.

The Law of Four

There is a "Law of Four" in negotiating. This law says that there are only four main issues that need to be discussed and resolved in the course of any negotiation. It also says that the opposing parties must have a different order of value and priority on these four issues for an agreement to take place.

For example, if one party is concerned about the price and the other party is concerned about the quality or the speed of delivery, then a negotiation can proceed to a satisfactory conclusion where a price is agreed upon in return for dependable, consistent delivery and quality. It is only when both parties are adamant about the same issue, like the price, that a stalemate can occur.

Your job, prior to giving a group presentation, is to identify the four major issues that you will eventually come to in the course of your discussion and then determine how you can offset, neutralize, or compensate for their major concerns so that you can be satisfied on your major concerns.

Presentation versus Negotiation: The Principles Remain the Same

When you make a presentation to a small group, the process may not be as lengthy or as dramatic as a two- or three-day negotiating session with huge amounts of money and egos at stake, but the principles remain the same. You must think through the concerns of the participants in the meeting and the four main issues on which you will have to get agreement if you want to proceed. You then design your entire presentation so that you achieve that goal at the end of the discussion.

Think on Paper

When making a business presentation, you should think on paper. Write down all the objections that an intelligent person could give you for not proceeding with your idea or accepting your recommendations. Then, write out one or more logical answers to each of those objections.

When the question, concern, or objection comes up, you should treat it with great respect and appear to think carefully about how you might best address that concern. Express acceptance, agreement, and appreciation. Then present your already carefully considered answer to the objection as though it just occurred to you in the last few seconds.

Always Appear Reasonable and Agreeable

Whatever the concern, resistance, or objection might be to your idea, always treat it with friendliness, courtesy, and grace. Never throw gasoline on the fire. The more low-key and friendly you are when you deal with the concerns or antagonisms of people in your meeting, the more open they will be to considering your ideas. Remember the lyrics "A spoonful of sugar makes the medicine go down."

When you give a small-group presentation, remember that it is not a dramatic monologue. It is a conversation. Present a point, wrap it up and summarize it, and then invite questions or comments from the participants.

Get Them Involved

The more you can involve the participants in the discussion as you go along, the better sense you will have for how they are thinking and feeling, and the more likely it is that they will agree with you at the end of your presentation.

There is a special feature of group dynamics that you need to include in your presentations. It is this: Each member of the group feels that you are personally treating him or her the same way that you are treating any other member of the group.

Group Solidarity

When you treat any member of the group with friendliness and respect, every member of the group feels as if she too is being treated with friendliness and respect. Each member of the group feels that he is part of a whole. On the other hand, if you treat any member of the group with irritation or impatience, the other members of the group feel that you are treating them the same way. Be careful.

Determine the Pecking Order

Even though you must treat everyone equally, when you make small-group presentations, you must be very alert to the "pecking order" of the members of the group. In many groups, one of the members is more important than the others. His or her opinion, expressed verbally or nonverbally, carries more weight than that of anyone else.

From the top person on down, there is a descending order of priority. Someone is first in importance. Someone is second; someone is third in importance. Some people attending the meeting will have little or no clout at all.

For you to make an effective presentation, you must be clear who carries the most weight and then organize your presentation so that you continually address the most powerful person in the group. In some cases, the top person will say very little. In other cases, the top person will say a lot.

Different Strokes

When I was in the Arabian Gulf recently, I read up on the negotiating techniques and strategies of people in the Arab world. What I learned was that in any meeting the person who sits quietly and says the least is the most powerful person in the room. The person who speaks the most and asks the most questions is the messenger boy and is often the least powerful or consequential in the negotiation. If I had not read that, the most talkative person might have unduly impressed me.

In western negotiating, the top person may say a lot or say a little. In any case, it is important that you know who this person is and that you defer to this person on a regular basis. You direct your comments to this person, and then sweep the room, making eye contact with the other important people, one at a time. You then come back to the top person and make sure that he or she is following you and understands the points that you are making.

Talking Is a Two-Way Street

There is a direct relationship between the amount of involvement in a conversation and the amount of commitment to the agreements made in the conversation. When you are talking with staff members, for example, the more you invite them to ask questions, comment, and agree or disagree, the more they will buy in to whatever decisions people make.

If people are not commenting or asking questions, they are not committing. They are merely listening. By not saying anything, they are avoiding participating in whatever decision is made and evading any responsibility for carrying out the decisions or the actions.

Alfred Sloan, one of the founders of General Motors, would often convene a group of executives to discuss a new company product or policy. At the end of the meeting, he would ask, "Are there any questions or comments on these ideas?" If no one said anything, or if everyone agreed with the ideas presented, Sloan would say, "Obviously the people in this room do not understand the importance of what we are discussing. If everyone is in agreement, then we must convene this meeting and reconvene at a later time. At that time, I expect comments and disagreements from the people around this table."

What Sloan found, and what many executives and presenters

find, is that if no one is saying anything, or if everyone is in agreement, no one has given the idea much thought. This means that
they will only start thinking about the ramifications of the discussion later, and this later thinking can sabotage the entire effort.

Take a Power Position

When making a presentation to a small group, organize the room
so that you have your back to a wall and the entrance is opposite
you. With this setup, people can come and go without breaking
up the flow of the meeting, and you can see each of them.

The best setup for a small-group presentation is a "U" shape
in which you stand and present at the open end of the "U." All of
the participants should sit around the outside of the "U" shape
so that almost everyone can see almost everyone else, eye-to-eye,
across the tables.

This setup is totally different from one in which everyone sits
facing you but next to, in front of, or behind the other participants.
There is little or no communication or opportunity to share ideas,
even by smiling, raising eyebrows, shrugging shoulders, and so on.
Always try to set up the room so that everyone can see everyone
else and see you as well.

When I conduct a strategic-planning session, I put all the executives on the outside of a "U"-shaped table. When I bring up a
point or question, I go around the table, person by person, and
invite him to answer or comment. This method has been extraordinarily successful for me over the years. It gives every single person a chance to voice her ideas or concerns, and gives every other
person a chance to watch and listen to the speaker express his or
her thoughts. By the time we go around the table, we have had

a rich, in-depth discussion that has covered a large number of points.

Determine the Next Action

Remember, the purpose of a presentation, large or small, is to agree on an action of some kind. As the conversation evolves, you should be continually asking, "What action do we take at this point? What action should we take on this issue? What is our next action if we are in agreement to this?"

When you are making a group presentation and a series of different actions is required, it is essential to get agreement from the group about exactly who is going to be responsible for the action and when it will be completed. Many excellent presentations that end with agreement on a course of action result in nothing happening. This is always because no one was assigned specific responsibilities with a deadline for carrying out the actions that were agreed upon.

Even if you have to repeat yourself or be a little demanding or assertive, it is essential that you get agreement on who is going to do what and by when if you are running the presentation. It is the ultimate goal of the presentation and the meeting. Your ability to follow up and ensure that these actions are taken is what gives the planning and the presentation value.

Make It Visual as Well as Auditory

In any group of people, about 70 percent of the participants will be visual in orientation. The other 30 percent will be auditory. What this means is that 70 percent of the audience, the visuals, will need to *see* the facts, points, and illustrations in order to understand and process what you are saying. The other 30 percent, the auditories, will be able to understand and process the information by simply hearing it from you.

As a result, 70 percent of your audience will probably only understand you if you illustrate what you are saying. Write down your presentation agenda so these people can follow along. You could use PowerPoint for your key points, bringing them up on the screen one at a time as you make the points in your presentation.

You can use a whiteboard or a flip chart to write down key points or to illustrate the ramifications and results of your presentation. People who are visual in orientation relax and take comfort when they can "see" your presentation unfolding. Auditories, on the other hand, are quite content with written or graphic material, but they very much like to hear what you have to say and will often ask questions about your specific meaning for a particular word or phrase. Be prepared.

Show, Tell, and Ask Questions

When I began to give seminar presentations, I started off using flip charts, then moved to a whiteboard, and now I use an overhead projector or a device called an ELMO. This allows me to write down my key points while they are projected on a screen behind or next to me.

As I go through my presentation, I draw graphs, pictures, stick figures, and other illustrations to offer a visual representation of the key points I am making. When I emphasize a particular word or concept, I write it down clearly so that people can see it.

As a result, people take an enormous amount of notes. As soon as you write something down, people immediately sense that it is important and they write it down as well. This keeps them actively engaged in your presentation throughout.

If you only speak, with no written materials or illustrations even the most brilliant mind will forget 80 percent to 90 percent of what you say before the end of your talk. When you speak and write, you capture both the *auditories* and the *visuals* and make your presentation an interesting and enjoyable experience for everyone in the room.

Understandings Prevent Misunderstandings

When you receive a question or comment from a participant in your audience, unless it is perfectly clear what the person is asking or what he means, you should do one of two things. First of all, you should rephrase the comment or question so that it is clear in your own mind before you respond to it. You can then say, "Is this the question you were asking?"

A second way to be sure that you are responding to the correct comment is to ask the participant to rephrase his question in such a way that you understand it better. Use the question, "How do you mean exactly?" whenever there is any lack of clarity or ambiguity on your part. The dumbest thing you can do is to set off to answer the wrong question or respond to a comment that you misunderstood in the first place.

Summary

Resolve today to prepare thoroughly and be at your best in every group presentation. Remember that people who can influence your career are watching and evaluating your performance.

Each time you open your mouth in a group, to persuade, contribute, or disagree, you are moving yourself forward or backward. And everything counts!

CHAPTER 7

Platform Mastery: Impressing Large Audiences

Dream lofty dreams, and as you dream, so shall you become. Your Vision is the promise of what you shall one day be.

—JAMES ALLEN

Once upon a time, a meeting planner phoned a professional speaker to enquire into booking him for an upcoming event. The planner's first question was, "How much do you charge?" The speaker replied, "It depends on the length of the talk that you want me to give and the amount of time that it takes for preparation."

The meeting planner then asked, "How much would you

charge for a 30-minute talk, and how long would it take to prepare?" The speaker replied, "For a 30-minute talk it would require six to eight hours to prepare, and the fee would be $5,000."

The meeting planner was surprised. "How much would you charge for a half-day talk, and how long would it take to prepare?" he asked.

The speaker replied, "For a half-day talk, it would take about three to four hours to prepare and it would cost $4,000."

"What about a full-day talk? How much is that?"

"That would only cost $3,000."

"How long would you require to prepare?" asked the meeting planner.

"Oh," said the speaker, "If it is a full-day talk, I can start now."

The Shorter the Talk, the More Difficult

My point in the preceding story is that the shorter the talk, the greater the preparation and precision you need to deliver the talk within the time constraints allotted. If you have all day to speak, you can fill the time with stories, examples, and various points that revolve around your subject. If you have only 20 minutes, you must deliberately focus and concentrate on only those key elements that are necessary to get your message across.

My first audience contained seven people, but over the years I have spoken live to as many as 25,000 people at a time. On one occasion, I spoke to 85,000 people at one time, with 2,000 people in the audience and 83,000 others in 600 locations via satellite hookup. The lengths of my talks and seminars range from 20 minutes to three and four days.

Every talk that I have given, either one time only or repeatedly, has required detailed preparation and practice in order to deliver it effectively and well. As your audience size grows, the requirements and demands of yourself as a speaker increase. Speaking to large audiences is very different from speaking to smaller groups.

The Eight Parts of a Keynote Talk

As I described in Chapter 1, there are eight parts of a keynote talk of 20–60 minutes to a large group. You can use this model to plan and organize your remarks. Let me touch on these points once more.

1. *The Opening.* This is where you grab the attention of the audience members, get them to focus on you, and make them look forward to your coming remarks.
2. *The Introduction.* This is your transition into the first point of your talk.
3. *The First Point.* This is where you begin to build your case.
4. *The Transition into the Next Point.* This is where you indicate that you are making a transition from the first point to the second point.
5. *The Second Key Point.* This follows naturally from your first point and builds on it.
6. *Another Transition.* This is where you shift into your third point.
7. *The Third Key Point.* This follows naturally from your first and second points.
8. *The Summary.* This is where you wrap up your talk with a strong call to action.

The Seven Essential Elements of a Speech

There is a proven recipe or formula that you can use to design and present a speech on any subject to any audience. Each talk can be graded on a scale of 1 to 10 on each of these seven parts. Whenever the speaker has a low score in one of these areas, it undermines the effectiveness of the entire talk.

Introduction and Opening

It is essential that you make a good first impression when you stand up to speak. As it happens, making a good first impression begins well before your speech.

Preparation is the key. Start by taking a pad of paper and writing out your speech, word for word. Use the "Down-Dump Method" I described in Chapter 2. Write out the title of the talk at the top of the page and then write out every single point that you could make or include in this talk. Very often, this down-dump of ideas fills up two or three pages.

After you have completed the down-dump, review the various points and begin to put them in sequence, clustering them around your major points. Record your entire talk and have it typed out double-spaced for you to review. Edit and polish the talk several times until you are happy with the sound, structure, and flow of the language. Once your talk is written out and you are satisfied with it, record it and then play it back, listening for parts that are unclear or that could be improved by rewriting.

There are some other things you need to do to ensure that your talk begins well and that you make a good first impression.

Practice Makes Perfect

Many people feel that Lincoln's Gettysburg Address is perhaps the finest single piece of oratory in the English language. The story was that he wrote the address on the back of an envelope as he rode by train to the dedication of the cemetery at Gettysburg. The truth is somewhat different. It seems that Lincoln had given parts of the Gettysburg Address in other speeches for several months before he crystallized it into what became oratorical history. He had practiced with various sentences and phrases until he finally had a perfect speech.

Martin Luther King's "I have a dream" speech in Washington, D.C., is a wonderful and inspiring piece of oratory. But Martin Luther King had practiced delivering parts of that speech over and over again in the previous years. The final speech brought together the very best elements of many previous speeches.

Check Out the Facility
A second part of making a powerful first impression is for you to arrive early, preferably the day before, and then walk through and familiarize yourself with the entire setup.

Check the stage, the sound system, the lighting, and the seating of the audience (see Chapter 10 for more about what to look for). Never assume that someone else is going to care as much about the setup as you do. Remember, many of the people setting up meeting rooms for large and small audiences are minimum-wage workers whose sole aim is to get the job done and get out.

I know this first-hand because not long ago I was invited to give a 90-minute speech to 4,000 executives and staff of a fast-growing international company. It was a three-day conference and the company brought in a team of experts to set up the stage, side-screens, sound, lighting, and seating. I arrived at lunchtime in the middle of the second day. I arrived early, and I am glad I did.

My style of speaking includes writing notes on an overhead projector or an ELMO. I stand in the center of the stage with the projector to my right so that I can speak and illustrate my points as we go along, maintaining eye contact with the audience.

In this case, the crew had set up the ELMO to the side, at the back of the stage, and facing in the opposite direction from the audience. When I pointed out, as gently as possible, that this setup would force me to walk away and face away from the audience each time I made a point, they shrugged their shoulders. It just wasn't that important to them. I quickly had them reposition the ELMO so I was facing the audience when I spoke. The talk came off very well.

Mix with Your Audience

Prior to your talk, mingle with the meeting planners, your hosts, and if possible, some of the people who will be in your audience. Introduce yourself, ask them their names, and try to learn a little bit about them.

Audience participants always enjoy talking to the speaker and asking questions. Your goal is to get a sense for the audience participants. You want to know what they are thinking and feeling. Above all, you want them to feel that you and they are on the same level.

Listen to the Other Speakers

If your speech follows one or more other speeches, it is important that you arrive early and listen to the earlier speakers. It is essential that you know what has been said to this audience before you stand up to speak.

Sometimes I am booked to speak last thing in the morning, before lunch. My hosts will say, "You will be on at 11:00 A.M., so you don't have to be here until 10:30 A.M." In every case, however,

I will be in the room when the first speaker, usually an executive of the company, begins the first remarks of the day. When it is my turn to speak, after my introduction, I will refer to what previous speakers have said, especially if a senior executive has made a point about the business. I will compliment the observations and contributions of the previous speakers by saying something like, "When your president, Robert Wilson, spoke to you earlier, he made an extremely important point . . ."

This proves to the audience that you care enough to participate fully in the meeting, as they are doing.

There is another reason why you want to hear the previous speakers. If you don't know what they've said, you could find yourself saying something the audience has already heard or that contradicts a point that someone made prior to your talk.

For example, I remember giving a talk to 2,000 people in Chicago. My talk was after lunch but I made it a point to be in the room by 8:30 A.M. when the other speakers began. The first speaker gave a good talk on the theme of the convention and wrapped up with a funny story.

There was a 20-minute coffee break before the second speaker was introduced. The second speaker had not bothered to sit in on the first talk. He arrived just before he was scheduled to go on stage. His talk was also tied into the theme of the meeting and at the end, to the surprise of the audience, he wrapped up by telling the same story that the first speaker had used. This time there was a little bit of laughter and a certain amount of discomfort. You could see from the speaker's face that he was perplexed that so few people had laughed.

Then the worst thing that you can imagine happened. The third speaker, who had also not attended the talks given by the first two speakers, got up, gave his talk, and ended with the same story. This time, the audience was completely silent. Nobody thought the speaker was funny at all. In fact, it was clear to the audience that the speaker had not heard the earlier talks. You could see from the looks on the faces of the audience members that they had concluded that the speaker felt that he was too important to arrive early. As a result, he bombed completely.

Think on Your Feet
On several occasions, I planned my talk thoroughly in advance and then had to revise it quickly because of something that another speaker said just before I spoke. Sometimes speakers have used the same joke or story that I was going to use.

Meet Your Introducer
To ensure a strong introduction, meet and talk with your introducer. Be sure you have prepared a written introduction, in large print, for him to read. At the top of the page, write the words "Please read exactly as written." A poor introduction, badly read, can start you off on the wrong foot with any audience.

It is amazing how often people who are asked to introduce a speaker make no effort to read and rehearse the introduction before they stand up. They read it in a clumsy and awkward fashion, stumbling and making mistakes. The way that you can guard against disappointing the audience is to be sure that your introduction is so well written that the introducer cannot hurt you if he does a poor job of reading it.

Showtime!
When you are introduced, take a deep breath and walk boldly and confidently onto the stage. Thank the introducer by either shaking

hands or even giving him or her a hug, if it is appropriate. Turn and face the audience members squarely, smiling as if you are really happy to see them.

Remain silent for a few seconds, allowing the audience to settle down and center its attention on you. Let your eyes slowly sweep over the audience, dividing it into four sections or four quarters, with two quarters in front and two in the rear. Select someone in the center of each quarter to focus on and return regularly to that person.

Begin with a statement that immediately captures the audience's attention by addressing a common desire, concern, or problem of the audience. For example, when I speak to a business or sales audience, I will often start off by saying:

> I have some good news for you (pause). We are living at the very best time in human history (pause). More people are going to make more money in the years ahead than have been made in the last century. Your job is to be one of those people and my job is to show you how to get there.

With this type of an opening, I immediately capture the audience's interest, attention, and curiosity. People mentally and physically lean forward, eager to hear how to achieve this goal.

Getting Your Point Across

No matter what your speech or presentation is about, there are several things you must do to make sure your audience follows your logic, is engaged, and becomes open to your influence.

Link Each Point Back into the Story

Any time you use a story to get a point across, be sure to link it back to your point often. For example, by the time I deliver the introductory statement I just mentioned, everyone is leaning forward, eager to hear the rest of the story. I then might explain how Alexander led his army against Darius at the Battle of Arbela, defeated Darius with superior generalship despite ten-to-one odds, and went on to conquer most of the known world at that time.

For the rest of my talk, I would explain the leadership qualities of vision, courage, commitment, determination, innovation, and responsibility. By the end of the talk, each executive should see himself or herself as a potential Alexander, contesting great odds to achieve victory in competitive markets.

Activate Both Brains

Nobel Prize–winning research concludes that humans have both a left and a right brain. The left brain is logical, practical, analytical, factual, and unemotional. This is the part of the brain that we use to take in information of all kinds. The right brain, on the other hand, is activated by pictures, emotions, music, and stories.

People make decisions with their right brains. Your job is to activate and stimulate the right brains of your audiences as much as possible. The more you address your remarks and comments to the right brain, the more fully engaged the audience will be with you and with what you say. Remember the "Windshield-Wiper" method.

As you develop your talk using facts and stories, select a person in the center of each quarter of the audience and return regularly to that person. Select people who are smiling and positive, and who seem to be fully engaged in your message. Focus on these people, one at a time, and speak a complete sentence to them, as if they were the only person in the room. Then, sweep your eyes slowly to another person in another quarter of the room, and deliver a line directly to him or her.

Look Directly at People in the Audience

When you speak directly to a person, everyone behind that person, fanning out in a "V" shape, feels like you are speaking directly to him or her. When you speak to a person farther back in the room, the people behind that person feel that they are the center of your attention. The more that people feel you are speaking to and connecting directly with them, the more engaged they will be with you and with what you are saying.

Stand and Deliver

When speaking to a large audience, practice the "Stand and Deliver" method. Pick a three-foot-by-three-foot or five-foot-by-five-foot square and stay within that square. Discipline yourself not to move around over a wide area or rock back and forth. Avoid the tendency to step forward and backward continually. These motions are usually the result of nervousness. You can control them by being aware of them before you stand up to speak. Let your arms fall naturally at your sides. Do not fiddle or fumble with your clothing, and don't put your hands in your pockets. Bring your hands up naturally as you speak to make a point. Then let them fall again naturally to your sides.

Making Smooth Transitions

This is very much like shifting gears. When you have developed a point completely, you need to signal clearly to the audience that you are moving on to a new point. If you don't, audience members will become confused and think that your remarks somehow tie into something that you have just said. Your transitions can be as simple as, "The next point that I would like to touch on is . . ." Sometimes I will say, "Now, moving right along, I want to tell you about this . . ."

Deal with each point completely, wrap it up with a miniconclusion, and then move on. Do not return to a point that you have already discussed. This only confuses your audience.

Speak Extemporaneously

Sometimes when you are speaking, a perfect example, story, or piece of humor will jump into your mind. Because this is natural and spontaneous, it is a wonderful way to connect with your audience. Signal this extemporaneous point by saying something like, "I just thought of something that illustrates this perfectly . . ." You can also say, "Just last night on television someone was saying . . ."

Let the listeners know that you are digressing from the body of your talk. You can say, "Let me digress for a moment . . ." When you have finished the story, like shifting gears, transition back into the body of your talk. Sometimes I say, "Here is a quick sidebar on this subject . . ." or, "Here is something that just happened last week . . ."

Whatever you say and however you say it, your audience must feel that you are in complete control and that your talk has a beginning, a middle, and an end.

Discipline Yourself to Stay on Track

There are many speakers who are what I call "enthusiasts." They are positive, funny, and articulate. They are usually intelligent, experienced, and well informed. But their talks wander all over the place. They often start well, with an opening story or important point. From then on, they leap from point to point, going backward, forward, and sideways, and blurting out whatever thought, story, or joke pops into their minds along the way.

Often they are funny, likeable, and entertaining. Audiences laugh and applaud. But at the end, the audience has no real idea what the speaker was talking about or trying to convey. People leave feeling somehow disappointed, as if they had been invited for dinner and all they got was an appetizer.

Maintaining Coherence

There is a deep psychological desire for people to sense reason, logic, and order in the universe. This is called a "sense of coherence." When you give a talk that moves clearly from point to point, you satisfy this need. As a result, the audience feels relaxed and comfortable with you. They are interested and curious to see where you are going next.

In Chapter 2, I mentioned the speech-design method of drawing a series of large circles in a row from the top of a page to the bottom and having each circle represent a key point that you are going to touch on. With my sales audiences, I teach what I call the "Spine and Rib" method of asking questions and developing a sales presentation. The spine represents the individual vertebrae—the key points to make in a conversation. The ribs represent the digressions, stories, quotes, or illustrations to use to bring the major points to life or prove them to your audience.

Planning your talk so that you go from point to point, like a frog leaping from lily pad to lily pad, makes it easier for you to remember and more enjoyable for your audience to hear.

Write It out Word for Word

Writing out key sentences word for word enables you to make sure your point is phrased in such a way that it will have its greatest possible effect on your audience. Look at the difference between saying something like, "You can do anything you want," and expressing the same thought by saying, "What you can do in the future is limited only by your own imagination."

Use the Power of Three

One of the most powerful speech devices is to speak in threes. For some reason, the human mind is unduly affected when you explain or express something using three phrases.

For example, in the Gettysburg Address, Lincoln used the famous words "Of the people, by the people, for the people." John F. Kennedy's famous inaugural address contained the words "pay any price, bear any burden, meet any hardship."

So in my talks, I often say, "You have the ability, right now, to solve any problem, overcome any obstacle, and achieve any goal that you can set for yourself." The more time and thought you put into the phrases and sentences in your talks, the more powerful and persuasive you will be.

Some years ago, a friend was encouraging me to write a book. He made this wonderful statement: "Writing is something that you can't get worse at by doing." It is the same with speaking. You can only get better at speaking when you speak. That is why the key to success in speaking is, to paraphrase Elbert Hubbard, "To speak and speak and speak and speak, and speak and speak and speak."

Creating Audience Rapport

The more people like you, the more open they will be to being influenced and persuaded by you. As Willy Loman, in *Death of a Salesman*, said, "The most important thing is to be liked."

Nothing gets the audience more involved with your message than for you to smile and be warm and genial when you stand before them. The more you appear to be enjoying yourself, the more the audience will enjoy being with you. The more people like you, the more they will open up to you and be receptive to what you want them to do.

One of the most powerful ways to build audience involvement is for you to ask questions. Whenever you ask a person a question, he is conditioned to answer. Even if he does not know the answer, or if it is a trick question or rhetorical device, when you ask a question, you grab his attention. He searches his mind for the possible answer. He leans forward to hear from you what the answer might be.

For example, when I want to grab the attention of a business audience, I casually ask, "What is the highest-paid and most important work in America?"

First of all, the audience responds with silence. Then, people begin to call out possible answers: "Show business! Sales! Professional speaking! Sports!"

After they have taken a stab at the answer, I smile and say:

The highest-paid and most valuable work in America is thinking. This is because, of all things that people do, thinking has the greatest possible consequences. The better you think, the better decisions you make. The better decisions you make, the better actions you will take. The better actions you take, the better results you will get, and the better will be the quality of your life and work. Everything begins with thinking.

I then talk about some of the thinking tools and techniques of the most effective people in business and industry. Throughout my talk I loop back to the ways that top people in this business think in different situations. This theme, running like a thread through my talk, keeps people totally engaged.

Keeping Good Timing and Pacing

The best definition of a good talk to an audience of any size is "enthusiastic conversation."

Think of driving a car with a standard transmission rather than an automatic. You continually shift gears in your talk. You can go faster or slower. You can speak louder or softer. You can change the intensity of your voice from relaxed to almost passionate.

When you continually vary the tempo, speed, and volume of your words, pausing and then continuing, faster and then slower, you keep the audience as involved with you as they would be watching a NASCAR race. This makes whatever you are saying far more interesting and enjoyable for the listeners. They never get a chance to relax or to become bored. You are always changing some element of the talk. I will talk about this in Chapter 8.

When speaking to large audiences, you will almost invariably be asked to give shorter talks. Large audiences are most often gathered for conferences at which there are multiple speakers. Thus, they have tight time frames and the various talks have to fit into these constraints. For example, a friend of mind was recently booked to speak at an international convention and flown to Hong Kong to give a 12-minute talk on his particular subject. That was the precise amount of time that the convention organizers had allotted for this talk on their schedule.

The amount of information you include in your talk is determined by the amount of time you are given. The rule that I follow is that if I am asked to speak for up to 30 minutes, I build the talk around three key points. If I am asked to speak for up to one hour, I build the talk around five key points. If I am asked to speak for up to 90 minutes, I include seven key points. These guidelines give you a template with which you can develop any talk.

Summarizing and Closing

This is often the most important part of your talk—the part that will be remembered the longest. It must be planned and delivered with care.

The rule is that you should memorize your opening and closing so that you could wake up and deliver them from a sound sleep. Your closing remarks should be like a very clear period (if not an exclamation mark) at the end of a sentence.

The simplest way to close a talk is to summarize your key points by repeating them, one by one, and giving the natural conclusion that flows from your remarks.

Your final remarks are the "Call to action" that asks or tells the audience what you want it to do with the information you have just presented.

The most important principle is to end your talk with a "punch." Sometimes you can use the "rule of three" to conclude your remarks and make your final recommendations. Sometimes you can end with a quote or a poem. If appropriate, you can end with a joke that relates back to your story and emphasizes the main point you were trying to make. In Chapter 11, you will learn how to end with a bang.

When You Reach the End, Stop

When you finish your talk, stop speaking and stand silently, smiling at the audience.

When I was a younger speaker, at the end of my talks I would say, "Thank you," and immediately begin looking around to see how to get off the stage. Sometimes I would start shuffling or stacking up my written materials. I found later that this merely disconcerts or confuses the audience. Instead, I learned the discipline of standing perfectly still and smiling at the end of my talk, signaling that the talk was over and that it was now the audience's responsibility to acknowledge and respond.

Wait for It

Again and again, as I stood there silently, first one person would begin to clap, then another, and another. Soon the entire audience would be clapping. If you are an outstanding speaker, one person will stand up while continuing to clap. Then a person next to him, or behind him, will stand up. One by one, the audience members will rise to their feet, giving you a standing ovation. But you have to wait for it.

Special-Occasion Speaking

There will be times when you may be asked to speak on a special occasion, often with little notice or time for preparation. These can be important moments in your life and the lives of others, and they must be attended to with care and attention.

The five most common special occasion speeches are (1)

awards and congratulations; (2) introductions or thanks at a public event; (3) birthdays or anniversaries; (4) weddings; and (5) funerals. In each case, you should use all of your speaking skills to give an excellent speech.

1. *Awards and Congratulations.* Think through your remarks and write them down before you speak. Be clear about the purpose of the award and what the person has done to deserve it.

Everyone is watching your performance and taking note of what you say, especially the recipient of the award. The more important your position in the organization, the greater will be the impact of your words and the longer they will be remembered.

Whenever someone is acknowledged and congratulated in front of others, especially his or her peers, the occasion is a major event. By speaking with warmth, intelligence, and knowledge about the recipient's valuable accomplishment, you can have a major effect on the person and on all the others who are watching.

2. *Introductions or Thanks.* You may be asked to introduce the speaker at a public talk or association meeting. Take this responsibility seriously. Everyone is watching.

On many occasions, because of the time and attention given to the introduction of the speaker, the introduction itself is actually better than the speech. Many aspiring executives have put themselves on the fast track by giving an outstanding introduction to a senior executive or important industry speaker.

Some years ago, I was invited to introduce Barbara Bush, wife of former President George H. W. Bush, to a large audience. I prepared thoroughly and gave such a strong introduction that she got a standing ovation as she walked onto the stage. The President, who was watching, personally thanked me afterward. I never forgot it.

You may be asked to thank a speaker after a talk. In this case, keep notes of the key points covered by the speaker. When you go up to thank him or her, briefly recap what you felt were the most important points of the speech. "Thank you for that wonderful talk. We all enjoyed your remarks. What I most liked about what you said was . . ."

When you speak well on your feet in front of an audience, people automatically think that you are smarter, more articulate, and more competent than others. Don't blow it.

3. *Birthdays or Anniversaries.* These are major events in the lives of most people. When you are asked to speak or to give a toast, do your homework. Speak to the person in advance and ask her a little about her life. Ask others about her to discover little-known facts you can weave into your remarks.

When you speak, always be uplifting and congratulatory. Avoid jokes at the expense of the people you are talking about. Make them feel good about themselves. By so doing, you make everyone in attendance feel good about themselves as well.

4. *Weddings.* This is one of the most important occasions in a person's life and in the lives of the parents of the bride and groom. The things you say and the words you use will be remembered for years. Plan them with care.

Some years ago, I was invited to the wedding of the children of some very nice people. They were blue-collar workers with a limited budget. They asked their 23-year-old son, a mechanic, to propose the toast for his 25-year-old sister, who was getting married.

The wedding was a lot of fun, and everyone was drinking, laughing, and making jokes about the newlyweds and about being married, sometimes a bit off color. But when the brother got up to speak, it was immediately obvious that he took his job seriously. As he began to speak about his sister, everyone settled down. For 15 minutes he spoke about their lives together growing up and about what a wonderful woman she was.

He went back over the years and told little stories about their childhoods, their parents, and their experiences as brother and sister. By the time he raised his glass and proposed a toast to "a lifetime of love and happiness" there was not a dry eye in the room.

When you are asked to speak at a wedding, think about your words being timeless. Speak only about love, commitment, and lifelong happiness. Be glad for the bride and groom, and wish them all the best in their lives together. Your words mean a lot.

5. *Funerals.* You may be asked to give a eulogy at the funeral of a friend or family member. When you do, you must write out every word in advance, for two reasons. First, you will probably become quite emotional as you read it. If it is not written, you will lose your place and your composure. Second, if you have written it carefully, people will want copies of it to keep forever.

When you read the eulogy, go slowly and recite each word. It should not be more than five to eight minutes long.

In writing a eulogy, begin by talking about how the deceased was a good, loving, honest, caring person. Go on to talk about his or her family members and how important they were to him or her. Talk about some of the person's history and accomplishments. End with a statement of sorrow and regret, and that "we shall never forget his/her inspiration or contribution to our lives."

Offering the eulogy for someone is one of the most important talks you can ever give. Plan and prepare it with care.

Summary

Speaking in front of large audiences is one of the most challenging and exciting things that you will ever do. Thousands of speakers give talks to large audiences every day, all over the world. It is a learnable skill. Remember that how you deliver a speech is as important as the speech itself. When you learn to give excellent public talks, as the result of preparation and practice, you will become one of the most persuasive and influential people in your field.

CHAPTER 8

Vocal Mastery: Powerful Voice Techniques

He is the best orator who . . . teaches and delights, and moves the minds of his hearers.

—CICERO

When you speak, your voice is your most important tool. Fortunately you can learn to use your voice, like playing a musical instrument, to increase your power and persuasiveness in any conversation or speech.

Singers are famous for training their voices for hours each day, sometimes for months and years, to reach a higher level of quality and resonance. You must do the same. Powerful voices are deeper, more sonorous, and stronger. They are infused with energy and power. When you speak with strength and confidence, as though you know your subject and believe in the importance of the points you are making, your listeners will believe you and accept your point of view as well.

Slow Down

When you speak more slowly, your voice has more power and authority. Your listeners have an opportunity to absorb and reflect on what you are saying. You exude confidence. You lend your words greater importance. All powerful people speak slowly, enunciate clearly, and express themselves with confidence. Loud, confident speaking is powerful and moving.

When you speak too rapidly, however, your pitch increases, often to something squeaky and childlike. Thus, the impact of your words and your influence on the audience both decrease because listeners downgrade the importance or value of what the speaker is saying.

Energy Is Essential

The most important element of excellent speaking is energy. Speaking has been described as "enthusiastic conversation," projected at a higher level of energy, to more people, and over a greater distance.

Some years ago, I spoke to 3,000 people at a new hotel in Orlando. My talk was a major part of a four-day conference. Because the sound systems were new, they hooked me up with two separate microphones, just to be sure.

Within five minutes of beginning my talk, both microphones stopped working. But the room was jammed with people and the schedule was tight. I therefore resolved to speak without the microphones and project my voice so that the entire room could hear me.

Somehow, I was able to pull it off. For ninety minutes, I threw my voice to the back row of the room. Afterward, I was exhausted. It takes an incredible amount of energy to speak loudly for any period of time, let alone the 90 minutes scheduled for my presentation.

The good news was that the talk was well received. Copies of the presentation were reproduced and distributed to thousands of people.

Everyone Must Be Able to Hear

When you speak to an audience of any size, your goal is to project your voice to the people sitting in the row furthest from the stage. By projecting that far, you will capture the complete attention of everyone in between.

In every case, the sound system is your best friend. Test it out carefully in advance. Walk around the room to see if there are silent spots anywhere. Be sure that every zone in the room is properly wired for sound.

Take Nothing for Granted

Not long ago, I was giving a one-day seminar for about 800 people in Philadelphia. I had spoken in the same room in the past. The sound system had been checked out and seemed to work just fine.

But when I began speaking, the back half of the audience began waving their arms and complaining that they could not hear me clearly. As you can imagine, when half your audience is upset and complaining, it is hard to continue speaking calmly and confidently.

As it happened, the people in charge of the sound system had not turned on the speakers in the rear half of the room. They had simply forgotten. And when the seminar began, the sound people had disappeared into some other part of the hotel. This is common as well. It took half an hour to correct the problem. In the meantime, I almost had to shout the entire time.

The Sound System Is Critical

Some time ago, I was giving a seminar for 1,500 people in a convention center that I had spoken in several times over the years without any problems. On this occasion, the convention center staff had "sold" the seminar organizers into using the exhibit area for the seminar rather than the banquet area we had used in the past.

The difference between the two rooms was that the banquet area had carpeted floors and acoustic ceilings. The exhibit area had polished concrete floors and high, airplane hangar–like ceilings.

Because of this construction, which was designed for shows and exhibits, the room had no sound integrity at all. Every noise bounced off the floor and ceiling and collided with itself, creating echoes and unintelligible noise. When I began speaking, no one in the room, aside from the first few rows, could clearly understand what I was saying. A revolt broke out. People stood up and shouted. They left their seats to argue with the seminar organizer. It was chaos.

No Sound Integrity—No Speech!

The people from the convention center were called and brought
into the room. As is customary with convention staff, they denied
that there was any problem and then further denied that there
was anything they could do. We were stuck with the room and the
nonexistent sound system. We were also stuck with a room full of
irate businesspeople who had given up a day to attend this seminar, many of them having traveled long distances.

Because audience satisfaction is my highest concern, I made
an executive decision. After quickly conferring with the staff of the
convention center and determining that a carpeted room would
be available two weeks later, I announced to the audience that this
seminar was being canceled for today, and would be held again in
two weeks. As compensation for their inconvenience, we offered
to let each person who had paid to attend the seminar bring another person at no charge two weeks hence.

Some of the participants were considerably displeased, but
fortunately most of them, being salespeople and entrepreneurs,
rolled with the punches. They accepted that this was an irresolv-
able situation and agreed to come back in two weeks, which they
did. The next time, we were in a different room, the sound system
had been checked out thoroughly in advance, and the seminar
came off without a hitch.

Expect a Deficient Sound System

It is quite common for hotels and convention centers to install
cheap and ineffective sound systems. Toward the end of construction, almost all hotels are over budget. They continually look for
places where they can cut back on construction costs. The two

areas they settle on, over and over, are the sound system and the air conditioning system.

I never cease to be amazed at the number of hotels and meeting facilities that have inferior and inadequate air conditioning as well as poor sound systems.

Almost all the meeting planners and seminar organizers that I work with arrange to bring in their own speakers and sound systems. It may cost a little more money, but it is an insurance policy against a disappointed or irate audience.

Building Vocal Power

The human voice is like a muscle. It can be made stronger with exercise and use. Many people with weak voices have become powerful, confident speakers by building their voices over time with exercise.

One of the best techniques for building your vocal power is to read poetry aloud. Select a piece of poetry that you particularly enjoy, memorize it, and then recite it regularly as you drive or walk around. When you recite a piece of poetry, imagine that you are making a dramatic presentation in front of a large number of people. Put emotion, strength, emphasis, and energy into the words. Go slowly. Change the emphasis on each word in a line of poetry and thereby change the meaning of the line. Imagine that the words are like piano keys. As you recite a line of poetry, change the emphasis from word to word each time you read the line.

My favorite poet is Robert W. Service. His poems are more like verses with wonderful rhyming and alliteration. They are easy to learn and remember. Once you have committed them to memory, you can recite them to yourself, and to others, for the rest of your life.

Each time you recite a line of poetry, as if you were presenting it on the stage, you not only improve with that particular line, you actually become better as a speaker with all your other lines when you stand on the stage in front of an audience.

Another way to build vocal power is to read aloud plays, especially the monologues from Shakespeare. When I was in high school, I memorized Mark Antony's funeral oration for Caesar from Shakespeare's play *Julius Caesar*. I still remember and recite that oration to this day for practice and to warm up prior to a talk.

Record and Listen to Your Voice

As you develop your ability to speak powerfully, record yourself reading poetry or parts of plays onto a Dictaphone or tape recorder. Replay these recordings over and over, looking for ways to improve your pronunciation, delivery, and pacing.

When my company teaches presentation skills, we instruct the participants to stand up and share a story about any part of their lives with which they feel comfortable. Some people explain their jobs. Others talk about their children. Some recount a recent experience. We instruct the participants to speak loudly and forcefully and to use their hands and gestures to make their points with great emphasis.

We then videotape the brief presentations and play them back. In almost every case, the students are astonished. They had no idea how poorly they came across when they were speaking to a small group of people.

Public Speaking Is Not the Same as Having a Regular Conversation

The most common mistakes people make include limited voice projection, stumbling over words by trying to speak too fast, pausing too much or not at all, saying "um" continually, and using insecure or ineffectual body language.

When students are told to be more animated, energetic, and passionate about their subject, and they attempt this during the videotaped presentations, they are almost always amazed at how what they consider to be high levels of animation comes off as small, self-conscious movements.

Overdo It to Do It Well

To expand your vocal range in front of an audience, speak as loudly as you possibly can, almost shouting, on a key point. Expand your arms widely and then let them drop all the way down to your sides. When you see this on a video, you will always be amazed at how limited and self-contained it appears.

My wife, Barbara, was raised in a household where her father worked the graveyard shift and slept during the day. The children were continually admonished to "be quiet." They developed the habit of speaking in whispers and tiptoeing around the house throughout their childhoods.

When Barbara began learning how to speak in front of a group, she was encouraged to speak louder. She raised her voice to what she felt was a "shout." But when it was played back on the screen, her "shout" was just slightly above a conversational tone. She was amazed. When you videotape your own presentations, you will be amazed as well.

Review and Improve

One of the best ways to improve rapidly as a speaker is to video-tape your presentation and then review the videotape with someone who will give you honest feedback. Stop and start the video each 30 or 60 seconds. Discuss how you could have used your voice and body more effectively to make a particular point. Stop the video at certain points and repeat what you said, exactly as you would if you had another chance to give this same presentation.

Record Telephone Conversations

You can increase your level of vocal mastery by recording your side of telephone conversations and then listening to them afterward. You will be amazed at how ungrammatically, haltingly, and often confusingly, you speak on the phone. But the good news is that every time you record and play back your own voice, you will see and hear different ways that you can improve your delivery and articulation next time.

Pausing for Power

Perhaps the most powerful vocal technique you will ever learn in speaking is the "Power of the Pause."

In music, all the beauty is contained in the silences between the notes. In speaking, the drama and power of the speech is contained in the silences that you create as you move from point to point. This is an art that you can learn with practice.

Many speakers are nervous when they stand up in front of an audience. As a result, they speak faster, with a higher pitch to their voices, and without pausing. When you are more relaxed, you speak more slowly, pause regularly, and have a deeper, more authoritative tone of voice. There are four kinds of pauses you can use to put more power into your presentations.

1. *The Sense Pause.* Use this pause by stopping regularly at the end of a sentence or point to allow people to absorb the new information and to catch up with you.

Listeners cannot handle more than three sentences in a row without going into a form of mental overload. At that point, they become distracted and tune out. Their minds wander and they are only brought back to your talk when you do something that grabs their attention.

There is nothing so attention-grabbing as a pause. When you pause, you bring people up short. They mentally trip and fall into the silence that you have created. They immediately give you back their full attention. Each time you pause, you get them to recenter themselves on you and what you are saying.

2. *The Dramatic Pause.* Use this pause on a particular point that you want to make stick in listeners' minds. You can use a dramatic pause immediately before delivering an important point or immediately afterward to allow people to absorb the importance of what you just said.

3. *The Emphatic Pause.* Use this pause to emphasize a key point. For example, partway into a seminar, I will often stop and ask curiously, "Who is the most important person in this room?" I will then pause and wait for a few seconds while people grapple with the potential answer. Some people will say, "I am!" and some people will say, "You are." After a deliberate pause, I will then continue by saying, referring to everyone, "You're right! You are the most important person in this room."

I will then pause for a few seconds to let that statement sink in. I then continue, "You are the most important person in your entire world. You are important to all the people in your life. And how important you feel you are largely determines the quality of your life." I then go on to explain the importance of self-respect and self-esteem, and how a person thinks about herself determines the quality of her relationships with others in both her personal and business lives.

4. *Sentence-Completion Pause.* This is where you make a statement or quote a line with which everyone is familiar. When you give the first half of the line, the audience mentally leans forward to complete the sentence with you. This causes people to engage more closely with you and to listen with greater attentiveness to what you are saying.

When I talk about how business is becoming more competitive and that we must continually increase our own competence if we are going to survive, I say, "When the going gets tough, the tough . . ." Then I pause and wait while the people in the audience complete the sentence by saying, ". . . get going."

Whenever you use this technique, you must discipline yourself to stop and wait until the audience speaks up and completes the sentence. You then repeat the words to finish the thought. You will have the total attention of the audience.

Tone of Voice

When you want to emphasize a particular point, you speak louder and stronger. The greater strength and emphasis you put into a statement, the greater relevance and importance your listeners will give it. When you want to share something sensitive or emotional, drop your voice and speak in a more intimate tone.

In a good talk, your rate of speech will be faster and slower, louder and softer, and broken by a variety of different pauses for drama, emphasis, and to allow people to breathe and catch up with you. The more you vary the various vocal elements of your talk, the more interesting and enjoyable it will be for the audience, no matter what the subject.

The Physical Side of the Voice and Throat

Your voice is the instrument with which you speak and persuade. There are things that you can do to ensure that your voice and throat are performing at their very best.

Energy is essential for good speaking and voice projection. Before a short talk, you should eat lightly. This ensures that you are bright and alert when speaking and that your brain is functioning at its best.

Before a longer talk, such as a half-day or full-day seminar, it is essential to eat well. Protein is best. A solid-protein breakfast or lunch will give you energy to burn for four to five hours. Protein is brain food, and you need it to think and speak effectively. Your voice will remain strong and your mind will stay clear.

To ensure the best possible voice, only drink room-temperature water prior to and during your speech. Cold water, commonly served with ice cubes, can chill your vocal chords and decrease the amount of warmth in your voice.

There will be times when you have trouble with your voice. When you have a sore throat, it can be difficult to speak clearly and project to the last row in the audience. If this occurs, drink hot water with lots of honey and lemon juice. This miraculous combination has saved me on several occasions.

Because of long flights and short nights, I have a sore throat about once a year. But by continually sipping hot water with honey and lemon during my seminar, my throat remains clear and my voice remains strong. I have been able to speak for eight solid hours, from morning to evening, with a sore throat, by continually massaging my vocal chords with hot water, honey, and lemon juice. You should do the same.

Summary

Training and using your voice like a musical instrument, varying your tone and speed, allowing silences in your talk, and delivering to the back row of the audience will enable you to speak with power in every situation.

CHAPTER 9

Tricks of the Trade: Techniques of Master Speakers

One of the greatest satisfactions that one can ever have comes from the knowledge that he can do some one thing superlatively well.

—HORTENSE ODLUM

There are perhaps 10,000 full- and part-time speakers in America today who speak professionally. Twenty percent of these speakers earn fully 80 percent of the total fees paid in the speaking industry. This means that 2,000 of these speakers earn four times as much as the other 80 percent combined.

The top 20 percent of the top 20 percent of speakers—the top

four percent of professional speakers, approximately 400 people—
earn 80 percent of the speaking and training fees paid to the best
speakers.

The top 20 percent of the top 20 percent of the top 20 percent—approximately 0.8 percent of all speakers or about 80 people—earn $25,000 and more for as little as a 20-minute talk. They
are often fully booked and earn more than $1,000,000 per year.
Some make even more.

The average full-time speaker-trainer in America earns less
than $500 per day, although the best speakers on similar subjects
often earn $25,000, $50,000, and even $100,000 per talk.

What are the main differences between the lower-paid speakers and the astronomically paid speakers? This is something I have
studied and worked on for more than 25 years.

The Highest-Paid Speakers

To begin with, most of the highly paid speakers are "Marquee
Speakers." These are people who are famous and well-known for
some accomplishment in politics, sports, or business. Best-selling
authors often become highly paid marquee speakers as well, at
least for a while.

Most speakers are hired by meeting planners or senior executives to address organizations, associations, or business meetings.
The goal of the meeting planner is to attract as many people to
the convention or meeting as possible. Annual meetings for organizations are usually important sources of revenue for planners,
which use them to underwrite the operations of their organizations during the year. The bigger the name of the speaker, the
more people will register, pay the convention fees, and attend the
annual meeting.

General Norman Schwarzkopf headed the successful military operation "Desert Storm" in the 1991 Gulf War against Iraq. When he retired, he immediately became a top speaker on leadership. He began to receive as many as 1,000 invitations per year to speak to business and organizational groups throughout America, Canada, and the rest of the world. His fees were consistently in excess of $100,000 per talk.

When General Schwarzkopf retired from the Army, he walked down the street from his official retirement ceremony in New York and gave his first speech as a civilian. He earned more from that single luncheon talk than he earned in six months as the general in command of 330,000 troops in Desert Storm.

The Journeyman Speakers

The second level of speakers, well-paid but not necessarily famous, are those who speak very effectively on a subject of considerable importance to many companies and organizations. In many cases, they are industry experts who have been successful in their fields and then turned to professional speaking.

These are the *journeyman* speakers—those who speak on business, sales, management, leadership, personal and professional development, and the humorists. These people are booked over and over again because they please their audiences consistently, and their reputation spreads.

Two Qualities of Top Speakers

The best speakers, in either category, marquee or non-marquee, have two important qualities.

1. *High Levels of Energy and Vitality.* They engage in enthusiastic conversation with their audiences. They are warm,

friendly, and likeable. It is clear that they are happy to be there with the audience and that they enjoy sharing their ideas with people they treat as friends and colleagues.

2. *Excellent Content and Delivery.* Because listening to a speaker is a form of "infotainment" and people are always interested in hearing and learning new ideas, excellent speakers share excellent material with their listeners. Speakers only succeed long term if they give powerful and popular public presentations. People must come away nodding their heads and talking about what a great job the speaker did on her subject. They must be eager to hear the speaker again.

Other Things Top Speakers Do Well and Why You Should Do Them Well Too

Even if you have no intention of ever becoming a professional speaker, knowing what makes these people stand out to audiences is useful for learning how to be a better speaker in your own circles. Here are some of their rules.

Please the Meeting Planner

In the meetings industry, word of mouth is the single most important determinant of repeat bookings. Before a meeting planner will hire a speaker, especially an expensive speaker, the meeting planner must be convinced that this person will attract a lot of attendees and then please their audiences.

For that reason, in the speaking industry, we often say that the job of the speaker is to make the meeting planner look good. When the meeting planner hires an excellent speaker and the attendees are happy, the attendees compliment the senior executives on their choice of speaker. As a result, the meeting planner looks good and is often promoted or given a bonus. The speaker will usually be used again and be recommended to others.

For example, I once was booked to speak at the annual meeting of a Fortune 1000 corporation. The secretary to the president was a fan of mine and had talked at home about benefiting from my material, so she recommended me to be the keynote speaker at their upcoming meeting. The president had never heard of me and was reluctant to bring in someone he didn't know for a meeting that was so important. Nonetheless, she convinced him that I would be a good choice.

The talk went extremely well and I received a standing ovation. Some weeks later I received a letter from her telling me that her boss was so happy with my talk that she had been promoted to a managerial job and given a $4,000 raise.

The reputation of a speaker, positive or negative, spreads quickly. The rule is that you are only as good as your last speech. Before someone will book a professional speaker, he or she must be convinced that the boss and the audience will be pleased and satisfied with the result.

Meet Other Speakers

Even if your goal is just to speak effectively in your business or social circle, you should use top professionals as models to learn from. Like they do, you should attend every talk and seminar that you possibly can. Take notes. Observe how speakers interact with the audience before the seminar and how they deliver their speeches when they stand on their feet.

When you attend a speech or seminar of any kind, make every effort to meet and shake hands with the speaker personally. Thank him or her for coming. Tell the speaker that you are looking forward to what he or she has to say. There is something about this kind of personal contact that rubs off on you and helps you to become a better speaker yourself.

Spend Time Studying, Researching, and Preparing

There are several rules that marquee speakers and professional business speakers must follow to get to the highest levels of income and acclaim. First, as I have said repeatedly, top professional speakers prepare thoroughly. It is not uncommon for a speaker to spend 10 hours on reading, review, reorganization, and practice to give a one-hour talk.

Top speakers learn everything they can about the audience. They ask about the ages, occupations, and backgrounds of those who will attend. They ask about previous speakers who have addressed this group and what the audience liked or disliked about those speakers. They want to know about the incomes and responsibilities of their audience members.

Professionals study the brochures and other information from the company and review client websites carefully. They study the industry that the company or organization is in, and they familiarize themselves with the major events and trends in that industry.

Be Clear About Your Objective

Like a professional speaker, you want to achieve complete clarity about why the meeting planner hired them in the first place. Remember, the goal is to make the meeting planner look good, and you can only do this if you are absolutely clear about what the meeting planner wants you to accomplish.

I always ask my clients in advance what they would like people to say and do as a result of my talk. Once we are both clear on this subject, I organize my talk so as to achieve that goal. That becomes my measure of effectiveness.

Not long ago, a meeting planner, the president of a large organization, told me, "Your talk was the best I've heard in 18 years. You covered every single point we discussed on the telephone, exactly as you promised."

She went on to say that many other speakers had promised to customize their talks for this specific group, but never did it. There is a belief among many speakers that, "It is easier to get a new audience than it is to develop a new talk." People with this attitude simply reshuffle the same old ideas over and over, no matter who they are talking to. But they don't last long in the speaking industry.

Learn the Language

Every company and organization has a special language, complete with organizational history, culture, and current events. A good speaker seems so familiar with the company or organization that he or she is addressing that the listeners get the feeling that the speaker works personally in their company or industry.

Plan and Organize Your Material

Professional speakers plan and organize their talks well in advance. They continually write and rewrite their material, moving some remarks and comments forward or backward in the presentation. They are continually looking for ways to make their points in a more enjoyable and effective way.

Review and Rehearse

They review and rehearse their talk over and over, even if they have given this talk many times before. They never trust to memory or experience. Just as a pilot reviews every point on his checklist, every single time, the professional speaker reviews every single point in his talk, and continues doing this, right up to the moment of delivery.

Check out the Location

Top professionals arrive early and check out every detail of the room, just as a general would study every detail of the battlefield. They check the three most important factors: the sound, the lighting, and the temperature. On almost every occasion, one of those three critical elements will need to be changed or corrected in some way.

People say video cameras are meant to be focused on a single face. In speaking, the audience comes for one reason: to see the speaker's face. Everything else they can get by reading a book or listening to an audio program. The face of the speaker is the focal point and center of attention in the presentation.

This is why some room setups make me cringe. For instance, some hotels set up the stage in such a way that the speaker is almost standing in the dark. The lights are focused 10 or 15 feet away. When the president of the company gets up to speak, people in the audience can barely see his face. And often, no one seems to notice or care.

Get to Know the Audience

Professionals meet and greet the participants prior to the talk so that they can get to know them a little. They introduce themselves, ask what they do, and make small talk with them. When members of the audience see you mixing and mingling with others prior to the seminar, they automatically like you better and become a more positive and supportive audience. When you stand up, you have already won them over.

Learn the Names of the Key People

One of the most important things a professional does is to learn the names of the key people and then refer to them in the course of the talk. Sometimes, I put words into the mouths of the key people. I will say something like, "Your president, William Henry, is always emphasizing the importance of quality in everything you do or deliver to your customers."

I will have read this in an annual report, letter, or e-mail from the president, or heard the president mention it in his or her introductory remarks. People are always flattered when you refer to them in a positive way from the stage.

Know How to Get On and Get Off

Professionals plan their openings and closings thoroughly and rehearse them over and over. They know exactly how to "get on" and how to "get off."

They review their introductions with the introducers so that they are clear. The way that an introducer brings a speaker onto the stage sets the tone for the speaker. It cannot be left to chance.

This is why a good introduction is carefully written out so that it raises interest and expectancy when it is read.

Engage the Audience

Top speakers engage the audience from the first words. They may start with silence to center the audience or with an opening remark to grab attention. Often, I will move to the stage, stand silently for a few seconds, and then say warmly, "Thank you for being here. I promise you that you will really enjoy what I've got to say."

This opening answers the unspoken question of the audience, "I wonder if this is going to be a good presentation?" It is an immediate crowd pleaser. Everyone smiles and relaxes. With the first few words, their key question has been answered.

Top professionals keep the audience members on the edge of their seats. They achieve this by asking questions, pausing, and then delivering the answers. They make points and emphasize key ideas. They tell stories to illustrate their messages.

Treat Them as Friends

Top professionals treat the audience as friends. They smile as if they are glad to see the audience members and as if it is a real pleasure to have a chance to share ideas with them. The audience members know instantly if you like them and feel positively toward them. You achieve this feeling by being charming and by smiling warmly before you even open your mouth.

Use Every Speaking Method Possible

When they begin, the top speakers promise that what they are about to say will be really interesting and helpful. They often tell a story about someone who heard these same ideas and who made a major positive change in his or her life. Top speakers use a series of rhetorical devices and other methods that have been developed and used on the stage or in movies for many years.

They use silence to center the audience and to give the audience time to settle down, or to digest key points.They use pauses prior to key points or immediately afterward, to punctuate their delivery and emphasize key ideas. They ask questions continually. Because people are conditioned to answer questions, when the speaker asks a question, the audience members answer it, if only to themselves.

There is a saying in selling and speaking that the person who asks questions has control. When you ask a question, you grab the total attention of the audience members for the length of time it takes them to answer the question. Their minds lean into the question, especially if it is one that can have different answers.

Keep Shifting Gears

Telling is not selling. Keep shifting gears by asking questions and then by delivering answers. Use dramatic pauses and extended silences before or after key points. Use a dramatic pause in the middle of a sentence before you drive the main idea home.

Top professionals are masters of timing. They tell a story in parts, with pauses and drama, sometimes digressing to mention another idea, and then coming back to the story. They tell jokes the same way. The following story is an example of what I mean.

Many people refuse to accept responsibility for the situation they are in. It reminds me of the story of Ole and Sven, who were coming over from Sweden many years ago on an old freighter. The freighter ran into a heavy storm in the North Atlantic.

Ole runs to Sven and says, "Sven, Sven, the ship, she's breaking up, she's going down!"

Ole says, "What do we care? It's not our ship."

Well, everything that happens in this company is your ship.

Let It Sink In

Professionals tell stories that make a dramatic and thoughtful point, and they allow the story to sink in. They allow people to process the point they have made. They give people time. They watch their faces until it is clear that they understand you.

Similarly, when you tell a joke, it is very important that you do not "step on your lines." When the audience laughs, let them laugh until the laughter starts to die down. Only then do you continue on with your talk.

Audiences like to be entertained by a speaker. They enjoy laughing. Don't deprive them of the time they need to take for thought and introspection, or of the time that they laugh after you have said something funny.

Use Both Your Voice and Body

Professionals speak a little louder. This demonstrates confidence in what they are saying. They use their bodies more, moving their arms, nodding their heads, smiling, and being more animated.

For example, when you want to make an important point, expand your arms wide or increase your volume. When you want to suggest intimacy, hold your fingers and your hands together gently as you lean toward the audience.

Let your arms drop. When you are speaking, your natural

stance should be with your arms at your sides, rather than raised in the "Tyrannosaurus Rex" position.

You can touch your fingertips together lightly to emphasize key ideas. Keep your head and your chin up, signifying confidence in your words.

Especially, smile warmly at the audience. Twinkle like Santa Claus. Enjoy yourself. Have fun. Be happy. Speak as though this is a wonderful experience for you and that you are enjoying every minute.

Summary

In the final analysis, the only way to learn to speak is to speak and speak and speak and speak. When you prepare, practice, and rehearse over and over again, incorporating more and more of these professional speaking devices into your performance, you will soon become a spellbinding speaker who is invited back again and again and who will make more and more money for each appearance.

CHAPTER 10

Controlling Your Space

We cannot make it rain, but we can see to it that the rain falls on prepared soil.

—HENRI NOUWEN

One of the key determinants of your success as a speaker is the room in which you speak. You must inspect it carefully and prepare it as much as possible.

There are three key physical considerations in speaking. They are (1) sound; (2) light; and (3) temperature. These are the three areas where things always go wrong in a speaking engagement. You have heard of Murphy's Law, which says that whatever can go wrong, will go wrong. This law was probably discovered by people who give talks and seminars in hotels and convention facilities.

Know the Lies People Tell

The first rule to know when holding any kind of public speaking function is that hotels lie. I learned this when I first began speaking and I have seen it proved over and again, 90 percent of the time. *Hotels lie.*

It is almost as if the people who arrange facilities for conventions, seminars, and speeches have taken a special course in the various lies, distortions, and half-truths that they tell the meeting planners and speakers, especially on the day and at the moment of the presentation.

Fire Regulations

One of their favorites is "fire regulations." They always say that they cannot do or change something because of fire regulations. The fact is that they do not want to change anything about the room or the setup. Their claim of "fire regulations" is invariably false, but it intimidates the inexperienced meeting planner into acquiescence.

Whenever I hear this, I simply say, "My father is a fire inspector, and I am quite familiar with the fire regulations. Please show me where in the regulations it says you are not allowed to arrange the room in this way." This always stuns them. They immediately drop the excuse and begin to cooperate. I've seen this happen over and over again, in hundreds of facilities.

"It's Computer Controlled"

Another excuse that they give you is that "The lighting is computer controlled. There is nothing we can do about it until the engineer arrives."

For some reason the engineer is never on the premises or immediately available. He or she is at a meeting, away on vacation, or dealing with another emergency.

How to Deal with the Lies People Tell

The key to succeeding in organizing the facilities is for you to be friendly, polite, and charming but simultaneously gently insistent with the staff. Your goal must be not to get them mad at you early in the process. They are the only ones who can help you. But here are some things you can do to get some results.

Threaten Them If Necessary

One day, I was doing a seminar in Tampa, Florida. The room temperature was 80 degrees. People were perspiring, waving their seminar materials as fans, and generally unhappy and dissatisfied. They were starting to leave and ask for their money back on the way out.

I asked the organizer to call the hotel and have them turn the temperature down. She called them repeatedly, but to no avail. They gave all the usual excuses. "The engineer is working on it; it is computer controlled; we are doing everything we can."

Finally, at the break, I called the head office and told them that if the temperature did not come down and the air conditioner was not turned on within two minutes, we would cancel the seminar, refuse to pay for the room, and sue them for lost revenues. It was amazing. As I stood there, I could feel the air conditioning coming on. After pleading with them for two hours and listening to every excuse imaginable, as soon as we threatened not to pay, the air conditioning roared on and stayed on for the rest of the function.

Refuse to Pay

I always encourage my clients to call someone in charge and tell the person, "We will not pay for the room if the air conditioning or temperature is not adjusted immediately." In almost every case, all the technical difficulties that had been holding them back are suddenly resolved and the temperature is lowered or adjusted to the proper comfort level.

Check the Lighting

Lighting is very important in a seminar presentation. The total attention of the audience should be on your face, with only casual side-glances to your props. Remember that 70 percent of the people in your audience are "visuals." They can only process information if they can see it. The other 30 percent are "auditories." These are people who process information only when they can hear it clearly. Your job is to cater to and satisfy both groups.

Fifty percent of the time, the lighting will be wrong in some way when you arrive to do your presentation. For this reason, you always want to arrive early enough so that you can check out the lighting thoroughly before you go on stage. If something is wrong with the lighting when you begin to speak, it is almost impossible to make any changes afterward.

Where to Put the Lights

In stage or TV productions, people spend one or two days in advance just setting up the lights. They arrange the lighting and move it around so that there are no shadows on the stage or on the actors. They make sure that every single person is absolutely clear to every single participant in the audience, from every angle. This is the ideal.

As the speaker, you must be fully lit, 100 percent of the time from both sides so there are no shadows on your face. It is not unusual for the facility to have lights that beam on you from the top rather than from the front, shading out the bottom half of your face. This causes a negative audience reaction.

The Phantom of the Opera

On one speaking occasion at a hotel, we asked for additional lighting and the hotel told us (remember, hotels lie) that it could only find one spotlight. The hotel staff brought it into the room and set it up to one side at the rear of the audience. This spotlight shone on one half of my face, giving me a "Phantom of the Opera" look for my entire presentation.

The reaction from the audience was immediate and negative. People actually became angry. They criticized the talk and demanded their money back. They walked out. For some reason, the half-faced lighting made me look sinister and evil and the people reacted in a negative way. We never made the mistake of having only one light again.

Your Face Is All-Important

When I organize lighting for a seminar, I tell the technicians that a person in the back row should be able to see a zit on my face from where she is sitting. I emphasize that the lighting on the stage should be as bright as an operating theatre. They often nod and pretend to agree but secretly think that you don't know what you're talking about. You must therefore be insistent.

In many cases, the staff will set up your stage and podium for the convenience of the screens rather than to illuminate the speaker clearly. The staff members will say, "If we turn on all the lights, it will wash out the screen." Be alert to this because it happens all the time. Insist that you don't care how the screens look. The light on your face is what counts.

Check in Ahead of Time

I was giving a seminar in Irvine, California, a couple of years ago. My seminar was for the entire afternoon, and, as usual, I arrived in the middle of the morning so I could watch the previous speakers.

When I walked into the room, a first-class Hyatt hotel facility, it was only half lit. It was a form of semidarkness, almost like a nightclub. The speaker was visible in a hazy, distant sort of way. I was appalled.

I immediately brought one of the hotel staff members to the room. I said, "Is there any way you can turn up the lighting in this room?" He said, "Oh, did you want the lighting up full?"

When I said yes, he immediately went to a wall panel, touched a couple of buttons, and the whole room became fully lit, classroom style. It was a shock to me and to everyone in the audience. They had been straining to see and get the message of the speaker for the last two hours.

It's Not a Nightclub Performance

This has become a common refrain for me. Whenever I go to a speaking engagement, I tell them that I want all the lights on full. I tell them, "This is not a nightclub performance."

It is amazing to me how many professional lighting technicians think that the speaker wants the audience to be darkened while the speaker is so brightly lit that he or she cannot see people in the audience because of the glaring light in his eyes. The other problem with this is that the audience views the speaker more as an entertainer. People sit quietly to watch the performance, not wanting to make any noise. They do not respond or interact with the speaker. The audience sits almost like a mole peering out of its hole at the speaker lit up on the stage.

Remember, unless you are a professional entertainer in a nightclub, you want what is called "one hundred candle power at desk level." This means that the entire room should be as bright as a schoolroom. You want people to be able to see one another, see you clearly, and take notes on the subject you are discussing. This is essential for audience enjoyment and satisfaction.

Control the Room Setup

The people who set up the chairs and tables in any seminar function are not highly paid. Some of them cannot read the instructions that you have so laboriously discussed with the facility staff. Their goal is to get in, set up the chairs and tables as fast as possible, and get out before anybody asks them to make any changes.

Supervise the Room Setup

When we were conducting our own seminars around the country, we would always ask to be present when the room was being set up. We knew that there were a myriad of mistakes that they would make and we wanted to be able to catch them while the staff was still available to do the heavy lifting.

Countless times we were told that the room was being used for a function the night before and that the setup staff would arrive at 3:00 A.M. We would say, "Fine, then we will be here at 3:00 A.M. for the setup." Time after time, we would arrive at 3:00 A.M., and the room would already be set up. It would invariably be set up incorrectly and the staff was gone. It then became a major issue to get people back to reorganize the tables and chairs the way we had originally requested.

Never take this part of the speaking engagement for granted. We always write out clear instructions, with diagrams, which we mail and fax to the meeting planners. We then phone or meet with them personally and discuss the details point-for-point with them so that they are clear.

Take Nothing for Granted

But even when you have thoroughly explained exactly the way you want the room to be set up, in almost every case, people will disregard your instructions or misunderstand what you have asked for. This is why it is so important to be there early enough to check out everything and to make changes when necessary.

Part of the reason I have been successful as a speaker over the years is my almost obsessive concern for the comfort of the audience. From my very first seminar with seven people, I gave a lot of thought to the audience's ability to see me clearly and everything that I was writing. I set up and reorganized the chairs and tables to ensure maximum comfort and visibility.

As my audiences grew, my concern for their comfort never diminished. Eventually, I was conducting seminars for hundreds of people over several days. I became very sensitive to the small changes that cause the audience to be much happier with what I say.

Everyone Should See You Easily

Every person in the audience should be able to see you clearly from wherever he or she is sitting. This requires that, whenever possible, you organize the chairs in half-circles moving outward from the stage, very much like a performing arts theatre. If it is a much larger audience, all the seats along both sides should be angled at 45 degrees so that people sitting in those chairs are looking directly at the speaker without having to twist or turn.

The first row should be close enough for you to reach out and touch them, almost like the first row in a live-arts theatre, where the actors could reach out and touch audience members. The farther away the first row of participants is, the greater the distance across which you must project your energy in order to make contact with them.

Keep People Close and Close Together

Imagine that your energy is a form of electricity. You want to create an electric arc—an emotional and chemical connection with your audience. The closer the first row is, the easier it is to make that electrical connection, which then runs though the entire audience.

Whenever possible, do not allow a center aisle when you are speaking. When you speak to a center aisle, your energy runs right down the aisle and out the back of the room.

But when you have a solid row of people in front of you, your energy cascades into the first row, like a wave from the ocean. It splashes into the audience, connecting with people, row after row. Put your access and egress aisles on the sides so that people can get to and from their chairs, but never allow a center aisle, if you have the choice.

Move Them Forward

Many facilities think that you will value the room more if they spread the tables and chairs over the entire area. This is not true. People do not care how much room there is *behind* them. They only care about how much distance there is between themselves and the speaker on the stage.

In the theatre, the closer the seats are to the stage and to the actors or entertainers, the more expensive they are. There is a good reason for this. The closer the person is to the speaker, the more enjoyable it is to the audience member. There is more intensity, more pleasure, and more satisfaction in seeing the speaker up close and personal.

It is not uncommon for the meeting facility to put the first row of chairs or tables 10 or 20 feet back from the stage. I called this the "shouting across the street" model. This is where you have to really work hard and project higher amounts of energy to make contact with the first row of your audience. This is both difficult and unnecessary.

If you arrive early enough, you can ask the staff to bring the back row of tables or chairs up to the front. I have often required that they bring as many as three rows of chairs and tables to the front to fill it in. I want to be able to touch the people in the first row when I reach out with my hand.

Spread out the Chairs

One final point with regard to seating: The standard meeting facility, hotel, or conference seating arrangements were designed when the average person was thinner than people are today. For this reason, if the chairs are put shoulder to shoulder, next to one another—sometimes even locked together—most of the audience will be crushed by heavy people either to the right or to the left of them. They will be sitting with their shoulders hunched forward during your talk.

If you have any control over the way the chairs are set up, insist that the chairs be shaken loose and that there be four inches or more between each chair. This will ensure that the audience will be more comfortable, more relaxed, and more open to the quality of your message.

It is hard to connect with an audience that feels crushed together in chairs that are too small for them, especially if the first row is set up 20 or 30 feet away from where you are speaking. These may seem like small points to you, but they are major points for each person in your audience.

When the facility staff members start to complain about "fire regulations," just tell them that you've checked with the fire chief and this setup has been approved. That will stop them every time.

Control the Stage

Visibility is a critical factor in a talk or speech of any kind. The larger the audience, the higher your stage must be.

Here is the rule: The person in the back row must be able to see the top half of your body, from the waist up. Therefore, the bigger the audience and the farther back the chairs go, the higher must be your stage.

You will notice that in large theatres, the stage is quite high, even above the heads of the people in the first rows. There is a good reason for this. People come exclusively to see the actors or entertainers, especially from the waist up.

Some speakers like to get off the stage and walk around the audience. Personally I think this is cute but ineffective. Why? Because when the speaker is walking among the audience members, 80 percent or 90 percent of the audience cannot see the speaker and has no visible connection with his or her face. It may be entertaining for the people immediately surrounding the speaker, but it is largely lost on most of the audience participants.

Tune in to the Sound System

The sound systems in hotels and facilities have greatly improved over the years. Nonetheless, as I mentioned in Chapter 8, most facilities try to save money by installing cheap systems at the end of construction. They then recommend that meeting planners bring in their own sound systems or rent expensive sound systems from the hotel or convention facility. The full-volume sound systems then become a major profit center for the facility in which you are holding your talk.

Most of the seminar companies and professional organizations that I work with will hire and bring in their own sound people. This is always preferable, even though it is more expensive. Most people who work in hotels are unionized and don't really care that much about whether the sound system is adequate or clear for the speaker. It is a sad fact, but true.

Microphones

The best sound systems in use today consist of a small, skin-colored wire that hooks over your ear and comes along the side of your cheek. It is virtually invisible to the audience and it is as clear as a bell throughout the entire room. More and more, these systems are available to speakers.

The Lavalier

Today, the most common alternatives offered are lavalier microphones, either remote or wired. A wireless lavalier microphone is best. It clips on your tie or lapel, and a wire connects to another device that clips on your belt in the back. This device is connected to an amplifier that is controlled by a sound person at the side or the back of the room. This type of microphone enables you to walk around and use your hands freely. It is often called a "freedom microphone."

The second type of lavalier microphone, which I used to insist upon until technology advanced to its present state, is a hard-wired microphone. This is a microphone that is wired into the sound system by a long cord. This type of microphone has no distortion and is often excellent for a talk or seminar. If you have a long-enough cord on this type of a microphone, you can walk around freely.

The Hand-Held Microphone

This type of microphone is ideal if you are giving an introduction or if you are simply making a few remarks. If you are giving a lengthier presentation, a hand-held microphone eliminates the use of one hand. It forces you to make all of your gestures with a single hand and it interferes with your natural expressiveness during your talk.

If you use a hand-held microphone, be sure that you hold it close to your mouth but under your chin. You don't want it in your face in such a way that it blocks your face from the audience. Always hold it down, slightly below your chin, and hold it close so that your voice projects clearly.

Managing a Podium

For many business talks, you will be required to speak from behind a podium. This podium will have one or two microphones built in. It is essential that you adjust these microphones so they are as close to your mouth as possible. You then stand straight and lean forward slightly, speaking into the microphone so that everyone in the audience can hear you.

Speakers often stand too far back from podium microphones and are not aware that their voices are not being picked up throughout the room. It is essential to lean slightly forward.

Resist the temptation to lean on the podium. It gives you a sloppy, slouchy look and suggests a lack of certainty in what you are saying. You can use your hands to adjust your paper or notes, but otherwise let them hang by your sides or rise naturally to make points, without touching the lectern or podium at all.

Even better, stand next to the lectern while you are speaking, only walking behind it to glance at your notes. The more the audience can see your full body, the more it will enjoy your talk.

Using Visual Supports and Props

When I speak for more than 60 minutes, I always use some kind of visual prop or presentation to illustrate my key points. This is because 70 percent of the audience members only register what you say if they can see it. They have to see your ideas in writing.

My favorite tool is an overhead projector. I stand next to the projector and write on acetate sheets, which project onto a screen behind me. Each time I make an important point, I flip on the overhead projector and write the point down clearly. I leave it for a few seconds, turn off the projector, and continue my talk. I also use this method to create stick figures and other illustrations that bring my points to life.

Many people have criticized me for using such an old-fashioned method of illustration when PowerPoint is so readily available. Nonetheless, they are always amazed at how much more enjoyable a live presentation is, with each key word written down and the projector going on and off, than a PowerPoint presentation.

Death by PowerPoint

As I mentioned earlier, in the speaking industry we use the phrase "death by PowerPoint." The reason for this is that when Power-Point came out, too many people embraced it as the central prop for their presentations, and they forgot about their voices, words, and gestures. The PowerPoint carried the weight of the message, which it was never meant to do.

If you use PowerPoint or any prepared visuals, you should use them as tools that keep the focus of your audience on your face and personality. When I use PowerPoint to illustrate key points with small groups, I bring up one line at a time. I discuss that line and explain it before bringing up the second line or illustration. Never bring up an entire slide and then attempt to read through the slide. Everyone in the audience will be reading up and down while you are speaking—they will not be paying attention to you.

Face the Audience

When you use PowerPoint, be sure you have a laptop in front of you so that you can see what is projecting onto the screen behind you or beside you. Never look at or talk to the screen. Never turn away from the audience. Always keep audience eye contact during the presentation. When you have finished making a point and you want to elaborate on it verbally, push the "B" key and blank out the screen so that every eye comes back to you.

Remember the 5 x 5 Rule

Remember the 5 x 5 rule for PowerPoint: Never have more than five lines on a slide, and never have more than five words in each line. In addition, each of the words must be as large as possible to fill the line. People in the back row must be able to read the screen easily and absorb the key points of your presentation.

Remember that the PowerPoint is a prop—a support—not the main message. It is merely a tool to emphasize and reinforce the points you are making, especially when it comes to numbers.

Flip Charts and Whiteboards

With small audiences, you can use flip charts or whiteboards. But never forget that the focus must be on your face, gestures, and words. If you use a flip chart, prepare it in advance by writing your key points in pencil on the flip chart. These will be invisible to the audience but will allow you to write clearly and authoritatively, as if from memory.

When you use a flip chart, after you have made your point and people have had a chance to absorb the words, numbers, or illustrations that you have written or drawn, turn the page over so that you once more have a blank page. This helps the audience refocus on you.

Another way to use a flip chart is to write out your key points on alternate pages in advance. Be sure you have a clean sheet facing the audience before you begin. When you go to the flip chart for the first time, turn over the clean sheet and there will be your first set of points. When you turn over this sheet, there will be a second clean sheet, covering up the next set of points.

If you use a whiteboard, after you have finished making your key points, erase them so that the whiteboard is once again blank. Otherwise, your audience's eyes will be flicking back and forth, like a windshield wiper, between you and the words on the board.

In every case, you want the audience to come back to your face without being distracted by what is written or projected on the board or screen.

Check It out Carefully

If you are going to use PowerPoint or any kind of electrical device for your talk, it is essential that you arrive well in advance and check everything out before you get on the stage. You will be amazed at how often professional technicians will set things up incorrectly. You will be amazed at how often your simple instructions have been ignored or misunderstood. There is only one way to be sure that your presentation will go smoothly and that is for you to set it up and rehearse it in advance of actually taking the stage in front of a live audience.

Control the Temperature

Ninety percent of the times that you speak, the temperature in the room will be wrong. In some cases it will be too cool, but in most cases it will be too warm. The reason for this is simple: It costs money to generate the electricity that drives the air-conditioning system. Once a hotel has rented you a room, including the cost of utilities, its engineers are instructed to do everything possible to reduce the electricity allocation to your room. This means turning off the air conditioning as soon as possible or not turning it on at all.

I always emphasize the importance of ensuring that the room is cool when people enter in the morning. It never ceases to amaze me how many meeting rooms are 80 and 90 degrees at 6:00 A.M. and there is no one available to turn on the air conditioning. The meeting planners often have to shout and scream to get the facility managers to turn the air conditioning on.

Don't Trust the Facility's Staff

Here's an example of why you need to supervise the facility carefully. I was giving a seminar in Boca Raton some years ago. After shouting, screaming, arguing, pleading, and threatening, the staff finally turned on the air conditioning. The temperature was about 85 degrees and people were already arriving. Finally, when the seminar began, the temperature was down to about 75 degrees. As I stood up to speak, you could hear the air-conditioning system being shut off by the engineers. It went silent. The temperature immediately began to rise toward the 90-degree-plus temperatures outside. It was unbelievable!

The Ideal Room Temperature

The very best audience temperature is about 68 degrees Fahrenheit. Below that, the temperature is too cool and above that temperature, the brain does not function as well as it could. All over the world, you will have to argue, fight, plead, and threaten the hotel or convention center people to get them to make the room cool enough so that your audience is comfortable.

When you arrange for a meeting facility, put a clause into the contract specifying a maximum temperature of 68 degrees— something like, "No payment for this room will be required if the temperature goes above 68 degrees for more than five minutes."

Some friends of mine who conduct seminars nationwide use this clause and have standing thermometers spread around the room on the various participants' tables. They check these thermometers on a regular basis. If one of the thermometers goes above 68 degrees, they immediately call the hotel staff and point this out. They tell them that they have three more minutes before the room is free. They have saved thousands of dollars in facilities fees by using this device. Of course, the hotels hate them.

One last point: When the facility finally agrees to keep the temperature at 68 degrees, be sure to say, "Do not change this temperature unless you have specific permission from me personally." There are always people in the audience who have extremely thin skins. If the temperature is 75 degrees, which begins to become sweltering for most people, they will complain that it is too cool. These hypersensitive people sneak out, find a hotel staff person, demand that they turn up the temperature, and then sneak back into the room. Don't let this happen to you.

Summary

The meeting room and stage are critical tools for your performance. Every single element has a positive or negative effect on the impression you make on your audience, and everything counts.

Make up your own checklist regarding light, staging, sound,

and temperature. Go through this checklist with the meeting planner in advance, and arrive early so that you can go through this checklist once more with the staff.

Always expect that mistakes will be made. Always expect that the hotels will not tell you the truth. The signal that things are about to go wrong is when they use the code words, "Don't worry about a thing; we'll take care of that." For some reason, these words mean "Nothing is going to be done to comply with your request."

When in doubt, always ask to speak to the manager. This is your last recourse. Whereas the staff is just trying to get through the day, the manager is usually concerned about you using their facility again in the future. When in doubt, go higher.

When you have taken care of every single physical ingredient possible, no one will be aware of it except yourself. The audience members will not even know why it is that they are comfortable in their seats and that they can all see without twisting. They will not be aware that the temperature is comfortable and that the sound is clear. They will not know exactly why it is that they can see and enjoy you clearly from anywhere in the room. They will not be aware of these things at a conscious level, but subconsciously they will be grateful, and afterward they will compliment you on giving a great talk.

CHAPTER 11

End with a Bang: Leave Them Breathless!

Do your work with your whole heart and you will succeed—there is so little competition!

—ELBERT HUBBARD

A good talk or seminar is like a good play, movie, or song. It opens by arresting the listener's attention, develops point by point, and then ends strongly.

The words you say at the beginning, and especially at the end of your talk, will be remembered longer than almost any other part of your speech. Some of the great speeches of history have ended with powerful, stirring words that live on in memory.

For example, during World War II, Winston Churchill stirred the nation with his tribute to the pilots of the Royal Air Force, who were fighting and dying in aerial combat with the German Luftwaffe: "Never in human history have so many owed so much to so few." Here is some advice about how to create a strong ending.

Plan Your Ending Word for Word

To ensure that your conclusion is as powerful as it can be, you must plan it word for word.

When you ask yourself, "What is the purpose of this talk?" your answer should involve the actions that you want your listeners to take after hearing you speak on this subject. When you are clear about the end result you desire, it becomes much easier to design a conclusion that asks your listeners to take that action.

The best strategy for ending with a bang is to plan your close before you plan the rest of the speech. You then go back and design your opening so that it sets the stage for your conclusion. The body of your talk is where you present your ideas and make your case for what you want the audience to think, remember, and do after hearing you speak.

End with a Call to Action

It is especially important to tell the audience what you want it to do as a result of hearing you speak. A call to action is the best way to wrap up your talk with strength and power. Here is an example: "We have great challenges and great opportunities, and with your help, we will meet them and make this next year the best year in our history!"

Whatever you say, imagine an exclamation point at the end. As you approach the conclusion, pick up your energy and tempo.

Speak with strength and emphasis. Drive the final point home. Regardless of whether the audience participants agree with you or are willing to do what you ask, it should be perfectly clear to them what you are requesting.

Close with a Summary

There is a simple formula for any talk: Tell them what you are going to tell them. Tell them. Then, tell them what you told them. As you approach the end of your talk, you say something like, "Let me briefly restate these main points . . ." You then list your key points, one by one, and repeat them to the audience, showing how each of them links to the other points. Audiences appreciate a linear repetition of what they have just heard. This makes it clear that you are coming to the end of your talk.

Close with a Story

As you reach the end of your talk, you can say, "Let me tell you a story that illustrates what I have been talking about . . ." You then tell a brief story with a moral, and then tell the audience what the moral is. Don't leave it to them to figure out for themselves.

Often you can close with a story that illustrates your key points and then clearly links to the key message that you are making with your speech. Here is an example.

> Once upon a time, many years ago, two friends from the East decided to go west and make their fortunes prospecting for gold. They staked a claim in what appeared to be a promising area and began digging. For one full year, they worked seven days a week digging deeper and deeper on their claim, but all they found was worthless rock. Tired and discouraged, they sold their claim to an-

other prospector for a few dollars, packed up their bags, and returned to the East to get new jobs and start new lives.

They learned later that the prospector who bought their claim brought a mining engineer out to the property to assess its value. After some study, the engineer concluded that there was gold in the ground but that the other prospectors had been digging in the wrong direction. He predicted that if the new owner dug in a different direction, he would find gold.

Just two feet from where the two prospectors had given up the new miner hit a mother lode of gold that yielded more than 40 million dollars over the next few years. The two young miners had given up too soon largely because they did not have the expertise of a mining engineer to guide them.

When the two young men heard what happened, they made a decision that changed their lives and ultimately made them very successful. They resolved that for the rest of their careers they would try a little harder, dig a little deeper, and hire the services of the best experts in any business venture they entered into.

Ladies and gentleman, we are digging for gold as well. The potential ahead of us is unlimited. Let us share our knowledge with one another as a team, dig deeper, try harder, and never give up until we achieve success.

Make Them Laugh

You can close with humor. You can tell a joke that loops back into your subject and repeats the lesson or main point you are making with a story that makes everyone laugh.

During my talks on planning and persistence, I discuss the biggest enemy that we have, which is the tendency to follow the path of least resistance. I then tell this story:

Ole and Sven are out hunting in Minnesota and they shoot a deer. They begin dragging the deer back to the truck by the tail, but they keep slipping and losing both their grip and their balance.

A farmer comes along and asks them, "What are you boys doing?"

They reply, "We're dragging the deer back to the truck."

The farmer tells them, "You are not supposed to drag a deer by the tail. You're supposed to drag a deer by the handles that God has provided. They're called antlers. You're supposed to drag a deer by the antlers."

Ole and Sven say, "Thank you very much for the idea."

They begin pulling the deer by the antlers. After about five minutes, they are making rapid progress. Ole says to Sven, "Sven, the farmer was right. It goes a lot easier by the antlers."

Sven replies, "Ya Ole, but we're getting farther and farther from the truck."

After the laughter dies down, I say, "The majority of people in life are pulling the easy way, but they are getting further and further from the 'truck' of their real goals and objectives."

Make It Rhyme

You can close with a poem. There are many fine poems that contain messages that summarize the key points you want to make. You can select a poem that is moving, dramatic, or emotional.

Some years ago, I gave the eulogy at the funeral of a dear friend who had died of a brain tumor. In his youth he had been a pilot in World War II and he had never forgotten his experiences in North Africa. After speaking of the great contributions he had made to his family, friends, and community, I read the poem, "The Airman," which ended with the words, referring to an airman who had died: "He broke the bonds of earth and touched the face of God."

It was an excellent way to summarize the essence of a good man's life and end on a note of inspiration for those in attendance.

Close with Inspiration

You can end a talk with something inspirational as well. If you have given an uplifting talk, remember that hope is, and has always been, the main religion of mankind. People love to be motivated and inspired to be or do something different and better in the future.

Remember, everyone in your audience is dealing with problems, difficulties, challenges, disappointments, setbacks, and temporary failures. For this reason, everyone appreciates a story or poem of encouragement that gives them strength and courage.

For years, I ended seminars with the poem "Don't Quit," or "Carry On!" by Robert W. Service. It was always well received by the audience.

When you tell a story or recite a poem, you must become an actor. You have to slow down and add emotion and drama to your words. Practice all of the techniques in this book. Raise your voice on a key line of the poem, and then drop it when you are saying something that is intimate and emotional. Pick up the tempo occasionally as you go through the story or poem, but then slow down on the most memorable parts.

Especially, double the number of pauses you normally use in a conversation. Use dramatic pauses before or after a key part. Use sense pauses at the end of a line to allow the audience to digest the words and to catch up with you. Smile if the line is funny, and be serious if the line is more thought provoking or emotional.

When you come to the end of your talk, be sure to bring your voice up on the last line, rather than letting it drop. Remember the "exclamation point" at the end.

Make It Clear That You're Done

When you say your final words, it should be clear to everyone that you have ended. There should be no ambiguity or confusion in the mind of your audience. The audience members should know that this is the end.

Many speakers just allow their talks to wind down. They say something like, "Well, that just about covers it. Thank you." This isn't a good idea; it's not a powerful, authoritative ending and thus detracts from your credibility and influence.

When you have concluded, discipline yourself to stand perfectly still. Select a friendly face in the audience and look straight at that person. If it is appropriate, smile warmly at that person to signal that your speech has come to an end.

Resist the temptation to shuffle papers, fidget with your clothes or microphone, move forward, backward, or sideways, or do anything else except to stand solidly, like a tree.

Let Them Applaud

When you have finished your talk, the audience members will want to applaud. What they need from you is a clear signal that now is the time to begin clapping.

Some people will recognize sooner than others that you have concluded your remarks. In many cases, when you make your concluding comments and stop talking, the audience members will be completely silent. They may be unsure whether you are finished. They may be processing your final remarks and thinking them over. They may not know what to do until someone else does something.

In a few seconds, which will often feel like several minutes,

people will applaud. First one, then another, and then the entire audience will begin clapping. When someone begins to applaud, look directly at that person, smile, and mouth the words *thank you.*

As more and more people applaud, sweep slowly from person to person, nodding, smiling, and saying, "Thank you." Eventually the whole room will be clapping.

A Standing Ovation

If you have given a moving talk and really connected with your audience, someone will stand up and applaud. When this happens, encourage the others by looking directly at the clapper and saying, "Thank you." This will often prompt other members of the audience to stand. As people see others standing, they will stand up as well, applauding the whole time.

It is not uncommon for a speaker to conclude his or her remarks, stand silently, and have the entire audience sit silently in response. But as the speaker stands there comfortably, waiting for the audience to realize the talk is over, one by one people begin to applaud and often stand up one by one.

If the first row of audience members is close in front of you, step or lean forward and shake that person's hand when one of them stands up to applaud. Somehow, when you shake hands with one person in an audience, many other people in the audience feel that you are shaking their hands and congratulating them as well. They will then stand up and applaud. Soon the whole room will be standing and applauding.

Whether you receive a standing ovation or not, if your introducer comes back on to thank you on behalf of the audience, smile and shake his or her hand warmly. If it's appropriate, give the introducer a hug of thanks, wave in a friendly way to the audience, and then move aside and give the introducer the stage.

The Power of Speaking Well

Your ability to speak effectively in every business or social situation can have an extraordinary effect on your life. It can bring you to the attention of people who can help you and open doors for you. It can get you better jobs and get you promoted faster.

Most of all, your ability to give effective presentations, both to small and large groups, will increase your own feelings of self-esteem, self-respect, and personal pride. When you know you can influence and persuade others in a variety of ways, you will have a tremendous sense of personal power and accomplishment.

And the best news of all is that these skills are learnable with practice and repetition. There are no limits!

Summary

Your concluding words can have an inordinate impact on your audience. Carefully chosen, your words can cause your audience to think, feel, and act differently than they would have without your influence. Sometimes, you can change their lives.

CHAPTER 12

Making Persuasive Sales Presentations

Nothing happens until somebody sells something.

—RED MOTLEY

Everyone is in the business of selling. The only question is, how good are you at it? Most people are terrified of selling because of the high potential for rejection and failure involved with trying to get someone to buy something. As a result, the very thought of being "in sales" is traumatic for most people.

As I mentioned in Chapter 3, people fear failure and rejection. Because these fears can sometimes loom so largely in our thoughts and feelings, we actually structure much of our lives to avoid being put in situations where failure or rejection is possible.

People choose relationships where there is a high level of acceptance. People choose jobs where there is a low probability of failure or rejection. People choose their social relationships and associate with people who accept them "Just the way they are."

Persuasion Is the Key

Nonetheless, everyone is in sales of some kind. Everyone is concerned with persuading others to his or her point of view. Even if it is just getting your spouse to go out to dinner at a certain restaurant or getting your children to go to bed, everyone is in sales.

Of course, people don't think of themselves this way. For example, once I was addressing a roomful of senior accountants with a major international firm. The accounting firm had brought me in to speak on the techniques of persuasion. I started by asking, "How many people here are in sales?"

The room went completely silent. One of the reasons why accountants choose the accounting profession is that they will never have to sell anything to anyone, and the potential for rejection is very low. The very idea of selling never occurs to them.

I paused for a second and then said, "Perhaps I didn't ask the question clearly enough. How many people here are *really* in sales?"

After a few more seconds of silence, the senior executive of the organization caught on to what I was asking. He slowly raised his hand and then looked around. As the other accountants saw the top man with his hand up, one by one it dawned on them that they were in sales as well.

Everyone Is in Sales

I then asked, "How many of you are here because you have the ability to bring in new business for the firm? How much of your income and your promotability depends upon your ability to increase the number of clients of the firm and your annual billings?"

Without hesitation, they all raised their hands. "So," I said, "Everyone here is in sales. The only question is, how good are you at selling? In the next few minutes, I will give you some ideas that will help you to be far more persuasive in working with skeptical corporate clients than you might have been in the past."

Selling Yourself, Selling Your Ideas

Public speaking is a form of selling, and the principles that apply to making a sales presentation are many of the same principles that apply to speaking in public. After all, the more audience members like you and trust you, the lower their fears are of accepting your message. The more they trust you, the more open they are to your influence. When they trust you completely, they will follow any recommendations that you make. Like selling, the purpose of speaking to any one or any group is to persuade people to think and act differently than they would have in the absence of your influence.

You always have a choice: You can be persuasive and influential, or you can be docile and passive. You can get people to cooperate with you, or you can go along and cooperate with them. The choice is yours.

The good news is that selling is a *learnable* skill. All top salespeople today were once poor salespeople. Many people in the top 10 percent of sales today started in the bottom 10 percent. With practice and repetition you can learn the skills of selling—persuading, communicating, and influencing effectively. All sales skills are learnable.

Reduce Their Fear, Increase Your Effectiveness

I mentioned earlier that everyone fears being manipulated or taken advantage of. No one wants to be sold something that he doesn't want, need, can't use, or can't afford. No one wants to be talked into something that she will regret.

So whenever you approach a new prospect for your product, service, or idea, he or she is conditioned from past experience to be cautious, doubtful, and suspicious. You trigger an automatic fear of making a mistake. Your first job in the sales conversation is to reduce that fear and replace it with confidence.

Sometimes I ask my audience, "What is the most important word in selling and in social life? What is the one word that determines how much you sell, how fast you sell it, how much you earn, your standard of living, your lifestyle, and virtually everything you achieve in your work and in society?"

Almost invariably, there is a long silence. Then I tell them the answer: *"Credibility."* The most important word for success in public affairs, speaking, selling, and business is *credibility*. The more that people believe you, the more open they are to being persuaded by you.

Everything Affects Credibility

Imagine a teeter-totter. When you meet a customer for the first time, one end of this teeter-totter is very high. This represents the customer's fears of making a mistake in dealing with you. The other end of the teeter-totter is low. This is your level of credibility at the start.

Everything you do from the first moment of contact, on the phone, by e-mail, or personally affects this balance. It adds to or takes away from your level of credibility. Everything counts!

The way you speak, walk, talk, dress, shake hands, and interact with the prospect raises or lowers your credibility in some way. For a sale to take place, for the prospect to accept your recommendation, her fears must go down and your credibility must go up so high that she can deal with you with complete confidence.

We say that "everyone likes to buy, but no one likes to be sold." Everyone is skeptical, suspicious, and cautious with offers of any kind and in any attempts to persuade him to do or think something different from what he is already doing. Everyone has been burned in the past and is determined not to be burned again. The way you reduce these fears is by raising your credibility.

The Seven Steps to Effective Selling

The process of selling to one person or to a group consists of seven steps. When you speak to win in a selling situation, just as when you speak to an audience, you must bear these seven logical steps in mind. If you miss any one of them, your selling or persuasion effort will fail.

1. Prospecting

The first step in selling is prospecting—finding people who can and will buy your product or service within a reasonable period of time. Prospecting begins with you determining exactly who your ideal customer is. What is his or her age, occupation, education, position, and previous experience with what you are selling?

Companies spend fortunes in market research every year to determine exactly who is most likely to buy their products or services. Before you sell or speak, you must become absolutely clear about the audience you are attempting to persuade.

The Four Requirements of a Good Prospect

As with audiences of any kind, there are four requirements a prospect must have before he or she is open to being influenced by you (or to purchasing what you are selling).

First, the prospect must have a *pain* that has not been alleviated. The prospect must have a "felt dissatisfaction" or have an area of discomfort that is bothering him or making him unhappy. Before you begin selling, you should identify exactly what pain an ideal prospect would have that your product or service can take away.

Second, a good prospect is someone who has a *problem* that has not been solved. Sometimes, this problem is clear to the prospect. Sometimes it is unclear. And in some cases, it can be nonexistent. But in any case, you must define the problem that your product or service solves in a cost-effective way.

Third, the prospect has a *need* that has not yet been satisfied. She wants some sort of improvement in her life that your product can deliver. What is the need that your product or service fulfills?

Fourth, a good prospect is someone who has a *goal* that he has not yet achieved. Your job is to determine what goal or improvement your product or service enables your prospect to achieve in a timely and cost-effective way.

Prospects versus Suspects

In a sales presentation, the first thing you must do is to separate prospects from suspects. You need to ask questions to determine the prospect's pain, problem, need, or goal that your product or service can alleviate or take away. The rule is "no need, no sale."

But even in nonselling presentation situations (i.e., business meetings, company seminars, convention presentations), your opening remarks should address one or more of the "big four" and suggest that your answer or solution is in your coming remarks.

State the Problem Clearly at the Beginning

One of the most popular ways to open a talk where your goal is to get them to take action on a product, service, or experience is to say something like:

> According to the insurance industry, of 100 people working today, at age 65 one percent will be rich. Four percent will be well off. Fifteen percent will have some money put aside. The other 80 percent will be dead, broke, dependent on pensions, or still working. In the next few minutes, I am going to show you how you can be among that top 5 percent and have enough money so that you never have to worry about money again.

2. Establishing Rapport and Trust

You establish rapport by asking good questions about what the prospect is doing now in his or her personal and business life, and then listening intently to the answers.

You establish trust and gain influence by explaining how your product or service has helped other people in the same situation as the prospect or member of your audience.

Questions are very powerful in establishing rapport. By asking open, honest questions, you demonstrate to the prospect that you are interested in what he is thinking and feeling and that you care about his or her situation.

Listening builds trust. The more intently you listen to another person after asking him a question, the more he will like you, trust you, and be open to being influenced by you.

What Do Buyers Like?

The National Association of Purchasing Management, which is made up of thousands of executives whose job is to purchase billions of dollars worth of products and services for their companies, does a survey of its members each year. It asks them two questions: What do you like most about the salespeople who call on you? What do you like least about these salespeople?

Year after year, the answers come out the same. The professional purchasers say that they like salespeople who ask good questions, listen carefully to their answers, and try to help the purchasers make good buying decisions. Here's a typical answer to what purchasers say they like least about salespeople year after year: "The worst salespeople come in here and talk and talk about their products and services, never ask me any questions, and don't listen to me when I try to tell them what I need."

Listen to Your Prospects

Listening melts away distrust and suspicion, lowers the fears of the person or group you are talking to, and raises your credibility. When you become an excellent listener, people like you, trust you, and are open to being persuaded by you to buy your product or service.

Telling is not selling. It is only when you are asking questions that you are selling. It takes no intelligence to blather on about your product or service. But it takes tremendous intelligence to take a feature or benefit and phrase it as a question, causing the prospect to think about your product and what the answer might be.

Phrase a Statement as a Question

Instead of saying, "This photocopier produces an astounding 32 copies per minute," you say, "Do you know how many copies an average photocopier produces? It might surprise you to learn that it is only 18 copies. But this machine, because of the advanced technology we have developed, actually produces 32 copies per minute." When you present a piece of information after you have asked a question, it is vastly more powerful than if you just made a flat statement.

When I speak to audiences of any size, I continually ask questions and then wait for the answers. In many cases, audiences don't have the answers, but the dynamic tension of the silence that is created after you ask the question rivets their attention and gets them hanging on every word. It pulls them into your subject. I then tell them the answer as though it is an amazing fact. Audiences love this question-and-answer method of speaking and presenting information.

Focus on the Relationship

Theodore Leavitt of the Harvard Business School once said, "All selling in the twenty-first century will be relationship selling." What this means is that the quality of the relationship that you establish with the customer or audience is the most critical factor in determining how influential and persuasive you are.

That's because *emotions distort valuations.* The more a person likes you and trusts you, the better he perceives your product or service to be. When he likes you, he feels that what you are selling is of higher quality and worth more money. He is more forgiving of problems or small deficiencies in your product compared with your competitors'. The more he likes you, the more positively he will respond to everything you do and say.

3. Identifying Needs Accurately

The first two parts of the sales process, determining that this is a genuine prospect and establishing rapport and trust, will get you up to bat in the sales conversation. But it is only when you and the customer agree that the customer has a genuine and immediate need that your product or service can satisfy that the customer becomes interested in your product, service, or idea.

Never assume. Even if many of your customers have the same need, never assume that a particular customer has exactly the same need as other people you have spoken to.

Take the "Doctor of Selling" Approach

Position yourself as a "Doctor of Selling" in your sales work. If you go to any doctor in any area of specialization, the doctor will go through a three-part process every single time.

First, the doctor will conduct a thorough *examination*. He or she will take a variety of tests; check your blood pressure, pulse rate, and temperature; and ask you a series of questions about your condition in the present and immediate past.

Only after the doctor has completed this examination will he or she move to stage two, which is to make a tentative *diagnosis*. A good doctor will discuss the examination results and then ask you if these findings are consistent with your symptoms.

When you agree with the diagnosis, the doctor moves to stage three, which is the *prescription* or course of treatment. If a doctor were to meet you and immediately recommend a prescription or course of treatment without conducting a thorough examination and diagnosis, it would be considered medical malpractice.

Identify the Need First

By the same token, when you meet a prospect or speak to an audience and automatically assume that what they want and need is what you are selling before you have done an examination, you are committing sales malpractice.

When the prospect agrees that he has a *pain* that he wants to go away, a *problem* that he needs solved, a *need* that he wants satisfied, or a *goal* that he desires to achieve, only then can you present your product or service as the ideal choice for this prospect.

If you begin talking about your product or service before then, you will actually kill any interest the prospect might have. The prospect will "turn off" and lose interest in listening to your recommendations.

4. Making the Presentation

The fourth stage of selling is for you to present your product or service in a persuasive way as the ideal choice for this customer, all things considered. Your product or service does not have to be perfect. It simply has to be the best choice at this moment to enable the customer to solve his problem or achieve his goal.

A good presentation repeats the information discovered when you were identifying needs and then shows the prospect, step by step, how the problem can be solved or the goal achieved with your product or service. The presentation is not so much an act of trying to persuade the person, but rather an act of *showing* the customer that your product or service is the ideal choice to solve the problem or take away the pain.

During your presentation, as you present each feature and benefit of your solution, ask the customer if each of these makes sense to him. Good salespeople ask for feedback at every stage of the presentation. Poor salespeople race through the presentation, talking only about their features and benefits, and at the end they say, "Well, what do you think?"

When you don't give your prospective customer enough time to process the information you are presenting, he will have no choice but to say something like, "Well, it looks pretty good, let me think it over." He remains unconvinced. The words "I want to think it over" or "Let me think about it," are customer-speak for "Goodbye, forever."

People don't think it over. This is just a polite way of saying, "You went through your presentation far too fast for me, and I do not see why or how I should buy your product or service at this time. But thanks for coming in."

5. Answering Objections

The fifth stage of professional selling is to answer the prospect's questions, concerns, or objections. There are no sales without objections. Because of the wide range of experience that a prospect has had in the past, the prospect will almost always ask you a series of questions about price, terms, conditions, quality, competitive offerings, appropriateness, and utility.

The highest-paid salespeople in my experience are those who have thought through every logical objection that a customer might give and have developed a clear and convincing answer to each objection. When the customer brings up the objection, the salesperson acknowledges the objection, compliments the customer for bringing it up, and then explains how that objection is easily dealt with and why it is not a reason not to proceed.

Poor salespeople, on the other hand, wing it. When they hear an objection, they often become upset and angry and are unsure how to respond. As a result, they lose sale after sale.

6. Closing the Sale

The sixth part of selling is to close the sale. You close the sale by asking the customer to make a buying decision now.

In golf they say, "You drive for show, but you putt for dough." In selling, everything you have done up until now is the equivalent of "driving for show." Your ultimate success will be largely determined by your ability to help the customer overcome any hesitation or doubt and make a firm buying decision.

The Invitational Close

Perhaps the simplest way to close any sale is to ask, "Do you have any questions or concerns that I haven't covered?" When the prospect says, "No," you then use the Invitational Close to elicit a buying decision. You say, "Well then, why don't you give it a try?" If you are selling services, you would say, "Well then, why don't you give *us* a try?" If you are selling a hard product—an automobile, furniture, or even a house—you would first say, "How do you like this, so far?" When the customer says, "It looks pretty good," you say, "Well then, why don't you take it?" Or, "Why don't you buy it?"

The Invitational Close is the easiest close of all and is extremely effective when the prospect is convinced that he or she will get the benefits that he or she wants from what you are selling.

The Directive Close

Another powerful closing technique is the Directive Close. With the directive close, you again ask, "Do you have any questions or concerns that I haven't covered?"

When the customer says "no," you assume the customer has said "yes," and then say, "Well then, the next step is . . ." and you describe the plan of action to purchase and take possession of the product or service you are selling. For instance, you might say, "Well then, the next step is that I will need your signature on these two forms and a check for $2,995. I'll take this back to the office, complete the order, set up the account, and we'll deliver it next Wednesday afternoon. How does that sound to you?"

The power of the Directive Close is that you keep the initiative and maintain control of the conversation. You conclude the sale or transaction and wrap it up.

Closing Is an Art You Can Learn

In selling, many people actually get through the first five phases of selling and then when it is time to ask the customer to make a buying decision, they go into a form of semiparalysis, like a deer caught in the headlights. They freeze. Their heart rates increase. They become nervous and shaky. They tremble at the potential for rejection that goes along with asking the customer to buy their product or service.

But this is not for you. Your job is to learn how to close the sale and then to practice over and over, until you can ask for the order smoothly, efficiently, and calmly in every situation.

Ask for the Buying Decision

When I was selling a restaurant discount card from office to office some years ago, I would give an enthusiastic presentation. But when it came time to ask for the sale, I would freeze up completely. Then I would blurt out, "Well, what would you like to do?"

It seems that every customer said the same thing: "Well, it looks pretty good. Let me think about it. Call me back." After a few weeks, I had people all over the city *thinking about* my product. But the telephone never rang. Again, I soon learned that the words *let me think about it* or *why don't you call me back* were customer-speak for farewell.

One day, I had a revelation. I realized that the problem was not my product or the customer. It was me. My fear of asking a closing question was holding me back. I resolved that from that day forward, I would not be put off by a good prospect.

The next morning, I walked into a prospect's office and gave my presentation. He nodded and smiled and said, "Well, it looks pretty good. I'll take a look at it. Why don't you call me back?"

I summoned up my courage and said, "I don't make call backs." He looked up at me sharply and said, "What did you say?" I repeated, "I don't make call backs. You know everything you need to know to make a buying decision right now. Why don't you just take it?"

He then said those magic words that changed my sales career, "Well then, if you don't make call backs, I'll just take it right now." He signed the order form and gave me the money. I walked out of that office on cloud nine.

I immediately walked into the next office, gave my presentation, and when the prospect said, "It looks pretty good, why don't you call me back?" I said the same thing. "Sorry, I don't make call backs. You know everything you know to make a buying decision right now. Why don't you just take it?''

And he did, and so did the next customer and the next customer after that. From that moment on, I sold to almost everybody I spoke to. I sold more in a day than I was selling in a week before I began asking for the buying decision.

Rejection Is Not Personal

In retrospect, I realized that the problem was my fear and my inability to ask a closing question. In many cases with yourself and in your selling activities, your fear of rejection can become so great that it can cause you to fail even with a highly interested prospect.

One of the keys to overcoming rejection is to realize that rejection is not personal. If people are negative toward you or to what you are selling, it has nothing to do with your quality as a person and most likely not with the quality of what you are selling or offering. It has to do more with the prospect and the fact that he has been brought up in a commercial society where he has to reject commercial offers or he would be overwhelmed with purchase decisions. Rejection is not personal.

7. Resales and Referrals

The seventh step in selling is to get resales and referrals from your satisfied customers. To achieve this goal, you must take good care of your customers after the sale, especially immediately after they have made a buying decision.

Preventing Buyer's Remorse

It is right after the customer has decided to buy that she is most likely to experience buyer's remorse and change her mind. You must be prepared for this.

The best salespeople and customers give considerable thought to how they treat the customer after the sale. They are absolutely determined that the customer is so satisfied with not only the product, but the service and the way the product is delivered and installed, that the customer will buy again and recommend his friends.

The Easiest and Most Profitable Sales

It is 10 times easier to make a resale to a satisfied customer than to make a brand-new sale to someone who has never bought before. This means that it takes one tenth of the time, money, expense, and effort to make a resale than it does to start from the beginning and find a new customer. This is because you have already established a high level of credibility with the already-satisfied customer.

A referral from a satisfied customer is 15 times easier to sell to than a cold call where you start from scratch. This means that it takes only one-fifteenth the amount of time, money, and effort to sell to a referral. The reason is that when you call on someone to whom you have been referred, you piggyback on the credibility of the person who sent you. The customer already trusts you and believes in the quality of what you are selling. All you have to do is be crystal clear about the specific need or problem that the customer has, show him that your product or service will satisfy that need or solve that problem, and ask for the order.

Selling to Groups: Team Presentations

Many products and services today are complicated. Rather than a simple sale, where you call on a single decision maker and the

single decision maker makes the decision to buy your product or
service, you often have to present to several people at once.

When you have to make a team presentation, whether it is you
alone or you and other people in your company presenting to several others, there are some steps that you need to go through.

Find Out How the Buying Decision Is Made

First, identify the political structure within the prospect company
or organization. How are these decisions made? How have they
been made in the past? What are the primary considerations in
making a purchase decision in your business or industry, for your
product or service?

Just as each person has a buying strategy, each company has a
buying strategy. Sometimes they like to speak to a variety of different vendors. Some companies like to develop a high level of trust
and rapport with a single seller and then deal with that seller.
Often the political structure is such that several people want to
meet with the seller and feel comfortable that he or she is the right
person to satisfy their needs. Whatever the case, your job is to ask
your initial contact how this sort of decision is made in his or her
organization.

Identify the Key People

Prior to making a team presentation to another group, find out
who the other people in the meeting will be. Get their names, titles, and areas of concern. Even better, phone each of those people and ask them what they are most concerned about and what
they would like to accomplish in the meeting.

Remember, preparation is the mark of the professional. And

the most important preparation you do is to find out the need structures of the people you will be talking to. What do they consider most important in making or supporting a buying decision of this type?

Find Out Who Makes the Final Decision

In every team buying decision, there is one person who can say yes. All of the others can only say no. Your job is to identify the final decision maker—the one who can make or break the buying decision. Sometimes this person will be out in front and asking a lot of questions. Sometimes this person will sit quietly and allow other people to ask questions. But you must know who the final decision maker is and address your remarks to him or her throughout your presentation.

Discover the Key Benefit

In every buying decision, there is a key benefit or "hot button" that the customer must be convinced he will receive in order to buy.

You should ask someone in the company—before you meet with a team of people—"What is the one thing that the people in your company must be convinced of before they buy my product or service?"

Uncover the Key Objection

Discover the hurdle—the primary obstacle to making the sale. What is it that would hold the client back or cause the client not to buy from you at all?

The answer to this question will be based on the client's current needs and past experiences. If you have a friend in the company, you can ask "What is the major obstacle that would cause this sort of buying decision to be postponed or delayed?"

You must get the answers if you are going to make the sale. You must know exactly what the customer most wants and needs, and simultaneously, the one objection that would cause him or her to hesitate or to delay a buying decision. Then, you must emphasize the key benefit, over and over, while showing how the key obstacle or fear is removed in doing business with you.

Speaking Like a Professional Salesperson

When you present to an audience, especially if you are trying to get people to buy in to your recommendations, think about how you can use these seven parts of the professional selling process. They will help you develop greater clarity and effectiveness in your presentations.

Determine the pain the audience has that your recommendations can take away. Determine the problem the audience has that your recommendations can solve. Identify a need the audience has that your recommendations can satisfy or the goal that your recommendations can help achieve.

Build Rapport and Trust

Take some time at the beginning of your talk to establish rapport and trust. Ask the audience members questions and wait for them to answer, either aloud or to themselves. Be warm, friendly, genial, and obviously happy to be with the audience. This builds rapport and credibility and opens people up to the message that follows.

Clarify Their Needs

Help the audience members become clear about the needs they have. Remember, many prospects do not know at first that they have a need that your product or service can fulfill. It is only as you ask questions and make points that it dawns on them that they want and need what you are offering.

Present Your Ideas Clearly

Present your product or service as the ideal choice for the audience. You can suggest that there are two or three ways to satisfy the need or solve the problem, and then show how your recommendation is the very best for this group, at this time, all things considered.

Address Their Concerns

Bring up objections and concerns yourself by saying, "At this point, people often ask . . ." and bring up a primary objection or reason for not going ahead. Then say, "This question is very easily answered. What we do to satisfy this concern is . . ."

Deliver a Call to Action

At the end of your talk, ask the audience to do something. It is not enough to end your speech and just let it peter out. You must make a strong statement and ask people to do something that they might not have done in the absence of your recommendations. The action you want people to take right now must be clear to the members of the audience, just as it must be clear to customers. Talk to them about how much better off they will be after they have accepted your recommendations. This is the equivalent of focusing on resales and referrals.

In the final analysis, people change only because they feel they will be better off after than before. So your closing remarks should emphasize how much better things will be for the members of your audience after they accept your advice.

Summary

Every conversation is in some way a sales presentation, and like public speaking opportunities, each sales presentation is an attempt to persuade people to act differently than they would in the absence of your remarks. When you master the skills of sales presentation, you will be well on your way to becoming one of the top 10 percent of salespeople in your field.

Index